Aspects of Augustana and Swedish America

*Essays in Honor of
Dr. Conrad Bergendoff
on His 100th Year*

Edited by
RAYMOND JARVI

AUGUSTANA HISTORICAL SOCIETY ❧ 1995

AUGUSTANA HISTORICAL SOCIETY
PUBLICATION NO. 44

Also published as Volume XLVI, Number 3 of the *Swedish-American Historical Quarterly*

ISBN 910184-02-X

Printed in the United States of America
Thomson-Shore, Inc., Dexter, Michigan

CONTENTS

ASPECTS OF AUGUSTANA AND SWEDISH AMERICA
ESSAYS IN HONOR OF DR. CONRAD BERGENDOFF ON HIS 100TH YEAR

Conrad Bergendoff. (Courtesy of Augustana College Library, Special Collections.)

ASPECTS OF AUGUSTANA
AND SWEDISH AMERICA

ESSAYS IN HONOR OF
DR. CONRAD BERGENDOFF ON HIS 100TH YEAR

Introduction

1996 has somewhat arbitrarily been chosen to mark the sesquicentennial of mass Swedish immigration to the New World, and numerous events both in Sweden and on these shores are now in the planning stages and will focus attention on this anniversary next year. In the following expanded issue of the *Quarterly*, however, it is our privilege and great pleasure to celebrate the extraordinary life and contributions of one of our own, who himself has witnessed and played a leading and decisive role in the maintenance and development of the Swedish-American community for two-thirds of the duration of this forthcoming sesquicentennial, namely, Dr. Conrad Bergendoff. Born on 3 December 1895 in rural Nebraska of Swedish-American parentage; raised as an immigrant "pastor's kid" in Middletown, Connecticut; and educated at Augustana College and Theological Seminary in Rock Island, Illinois, as well as at several distinguished American and European universities, Dr. Bergendoff significantly began his career as a clergyman, serving from 1921 to 1931 as pastor of Salem Lutheran Church, an Augustana Synod congregation on the south side of Chicago.

When Dr. Bergendoff returned to Augustana as dean of the seminary in 1931, his credentials as a leading scholar of Church history had been solidly established by the appearance in print of his University of Chicago doctoral dissertation *Olavus Petri and the Ecclesiastical Transformation in Sweden (1521-1552): A Study in the Swedish Reformation* (1928; 2nd edn., 1965), a work that remains the standard English-language treatment of its subject. Augustana and the Quad Cities now became Dr. Bergendoff's abiding material, intellectual, and spiritual home; in 1931 he also affiliated with St. John's Lutheran Church in Rock Island, where he currently is enjoying his sixty-fourth year of membership. Promoted in 1935 from dean of the seminary to president of both schools, he now embarked on a twenty-seven-year phase of his career during which he not only sustained a personal setback when in 1948 the college and the theological seminary ceased to exist under the common name of Augustana but also—especially during the 1950s and early 1960s—provided the wise counsel and leadership that resulted in the development of Augustana College into a leading regional institution of higher education in the liberal arts.

Another aspect of Conrad Bergendoff's leadership is the key role he has played in the life and times of the Swedish-American Historical Society, even prior to its inception. After serving as president of the Swedish Pioneer Centennial of 1948, he gladly became one of the founders of the ongoing organization that was engendered by this celebration. From October 1948 until April 1983, it was called the Swedish Pioneer Historical Society; and the slogan that has appeared on the masthead of every single issue of the *Quarterly*: "Established to record the achievements of the Swedish Pioneers," was Conrad Bergendoff's suggestion. His service to the society has been exemplary and multifaceted: from 1950 until 1959, he was managing editor of our publications committee, on which he continued to serve until 1974; his tenure as a member of the executive board lasted from 1953 until 1965; and he served as president of the society from 1962 to 1965. He gave the keynote addresses at our twentieth- and thirtieth-anniversary banquets held respectively in 1968 and 1978. At the latter event, he was awarded our Carl Sandburg medal. Between 1954 and 1993, thirteen of his articles were published in the *Quarterly*; and he continues to enjoy life membership in the society.

The essays that follow all pertain to the common theme at the core of Dr. Bergendoff's life's work, i.e., education and religion in both the Swedish immigrant and the broader American communities. Strictly speaking, they are not being presented to Dr. Bergendoff as a *Festschrift*, since he already has been honored with an excellent suchlike volume, *The Swedish Immigrant Community in Transition*, edited by J. Iverne Dowie and Ernest M. Espelie (1963). But the essays at hand do indeed complement this *Festschrift*; for example, since 1963, Dr. Bergendoff has hardly been one to rest on his laurels—hence the need to provide a bibliography of his published writings between 1963 and 1995, which Judith Belan has compiled for publication in this special Bergendoff centennial issue of the *Quarterly*. We also wish to convey our sincere thanks to the Augustana

Historical Society for its substantive contributions to and financial support of this project.

To conclude this introduction on a personal note, I have gotten to know Dr. Bergendoff by studying his scholarship—to paraphrase Schopenhauer, reading is simply thinking with someone else's thoughts. Several years ago during a visit to the Jenny Lind Chapel in Andover, Illinois, I first head his voice by means of the tape-recorded commentary on the history of this Swedish-American landmark, which he has provided in flawless American Swedish. In 1992, I had the good fortune of preparing the text of his article "A Swedish University Tradition in America" for publication in the *Quarterly* (Vol. 44, No. 1, pp. 4-20). Finally on 29 April 1994—when he was 98 and I was 51—I met Dr. Bergendoff after the sixth O. Fritiof Ander lecture delivered that evening by Nils William Olsson at Augustana College. Conrad Bergendoff's kind words of gratitude for my editorial work on his behalf and the immediacy of his human engagement: these things remain an epiphany in the days of my life.

RAYMOND JARVI

THE MOSAIC OF AUGUSTANA'S SWEDISH LUTHERAN ORIGINS

EMMET E. EKLUND

In 1860 when the Augustana Lutheran Church was organized, America was a fluid, dynamic frontier society. Religious groups were established to serve the spiritual needs of the settlers of the new land. Many of these groups were rootless with little doctrinal substance, but they gave people spiritual strength for the difficult life on the frontier. Among these settlers were various Swedish pastors and laity. Some of them had come simply for adventure; others came out of dissatisfaction with life in Sweden. Included in the latter group were pastors who were displeased with the rigid, cold church life in the Old Country. They wanted to found a new church with spontaneity and closer ties to the people. Still they came with strong roots in the Lutheran Church of their homeland. These roots they neither could nor would deny. Rather they built a new church based on their Lutheran origins and fashioned it for its unique role in a pluralistic religious environment.

*

Three non-Lutheran groups strongly influenced religious life in nineteenth-century Sweden and ultimately Augustana in America; they were the Moravians (better known as Herrnhuters), Scottish Presbyterians, and English Methodists.

The great missionary movement, the father of which is generally regarded as the English Baptist William Carey (1761-1834), started in the last decade of the eighteenth century. Many years earlier, however, the Moravians began their notable missionary work in a number of lands, including Sweden. They came to this Nordic country as early as the 1730s. Sometime between 1731 and 1734, Sven Rosen, a Swedish layman who had been converted to the Moravian faith during his travels to Riga, began his work in Sweden. "Thereafter the Moravians were a continuous force in the development of pietism in Sweden."[1]   That the Moravians were tolerated in a religious climate which later on became hostile to Baptists and Methodists may have been due in part to their irenic spirit. Also, they found a relatively friendly reception in Sweden because they, together with their patron, Count Nikolaus Ludwig Zinzendorf (1700-1760), accepted the Augsburg Confession.

A second influence on the Augustana mosaic of Swedish Lutheran origins was Presbyterianism. In 1809, two Scottish colporteurs, John Patterson and Ebenezer Henderson, established in Sweden the Evangelical Society, the purpose of which was to distribute tracts and Bibles. These Scotsmen also organized the Gothenburg Bible Society in 1813, two years before the emergence of the better-known Swedish Bible Society. The latter was founded in 1815 and worked in close cooperation with the British and Foreign Bible Society.

Other significant influences of the Free Church of Scotland on Swedish life included the young Swedish pastor Hans Jacob Lundborg, who spent several months in Scotland in 1855. By that time, the Free Church of Scotland had been separated from the Scottish State Church for twelve years and had become a remarkable example of spiritual growth and vitality.

> Lundborg was impressed by the Scottish Free Church and he diligently devoted himself to learning as much as possible about its missionary activities, colleges, and Sunday schools. At the same time [he] was critical of the doctrinal basis of the Scottish Free Church. His own loyalty to the Lutheran confessions caused him to regard the Scottish Church as 'sectarian orthodoxy which sought unity [of the church] in form and constitution before there was unity in faith and love.' Still Lundborg was strongly attracted to the spiritual life he witnessed in Scotland, and he believed that Sweden itself could benefit from the Scottish example.[2]

It was the form and spirit, not the doctrinal substance of the Free Church of Scotland, that shaped the determination of Lundborg to found a religious society upon his return to Sweden. In 1856, Lundborg became one of the organizers of *Evangeliska Fosterlandsstiftelsen*. The founders resolved that their society was to be true to the Lutheran confessions and was to work within the Church of Sweden but at the same time exercise an independence similar to that of the Free Church of Scotland, which had so deeply impressed

Lundborg. *Evangeliska Fosterlandsstiftelsen* gave overall direction "to the revival and temperance movement throughout the land, [published and distributed] devotional literature and portions of the Scripture . . . [trained and sent out] lay evangelists and colporteurs . . . and [set in motion and gave moral and financial support to] missionary projects of various kinds."[3] The pioneer pastors of the Augustana Church were in close correspondence with this society and received some financial aid from it.

Evangeliska Fosterlandsstiftelsen also possessed two characteristics that bore striking resemblance to the Augustana Church. On the one hand, it was an organization that was free from the established Church of Sweden; on the other, it was in association with it in its doctrinal and confessional stance. Such was the situation of Augustana, although its freedom was not so consciously formed as was that of *Evangeliska Fosterlandsstiftelsen*. Augustana's independence resulted in part from the generally negative attitude it suffered early on from the Church of Sweden. Also, necessary freedoms were imposed upon it by the First Amendment of the American Constitution with its separation of church and state.

One final aspect of the impact of Scottish Presbyterianism is the admiration of its Free Church by a group of Swedish pastors led by Hans Birger Hammar and Carl Bergman. They founded an organization called the "Society for the Advancement of Religious Freedom." Tufve Nilsson Hasselquist was active in this organization before he came to America in 1852. It is true that the Augustana constitution formulated by Lars Paul Esbjörn with the assistance of Erland Carlsson "followed in the main the constitution of the Synod of Northern Illinois, with some significant changes."[4] Yet, we may assume that Hasselquist, on the basis of his active membership in the Swedish Society for the Advancement of Religious Freedom, exerted an important influence in the framing of Augustana's constitution.

Along with the impact of the Moravians and Presbyterian Scotland on the mosaic of Augustana, was the Methodist movement, which was initially brought to Sweden in 1830 by George Scott (1804-1874). Born in Edinburgh, Scotland, he left its State Presbyterian Church and joined the Wesleyan Methodists. First a lay preacher, he was ordained a Methodist minister in 1828, and in the autumn of 1830 he went to Sweden. He was sent there by the English industrialist Samuel Owens to minister to the latter's English workers in that Nordic country. Of a tolerant nature, Scott learned to speak Swedish fluently. Bethlehem Chapel in Stockholm became the hub of his activities. He conducted a vital ministry in evangelism, temperance, and colportage. He would spend more than an decade in Sweden, but was forced to flee in 1842 because of injudicious and negative comments he had made the previous year on a tour in America about the quality of the religious life in this Nordic land.

During the 1830s, Carl Olof Rosenius was studying theology at Uppsala University. He was troubled about his spiritual life, and in his search for peace with God he sought out George Scott. "Through the ministry of Scott, Rosenius was brought to spiritual clarity and an unshakable faith in God and His Word. He soon became the intimate friend and most trusted helper of Scott."[5] On the recommendation of George Scott, Rosenius was granted an annual salary from the Foreign Evangelical Society of New York City and began serving as a city missionary in Stockholm. This stipend enabled Rosenius to work as an evangelist without the precondition of being ordained.

Moravians, Scottish Presbyterians, and English Methodists: here figuratively is the first characteristic of a mosaic, defined by Webster as an "inlaid work composed of bits of stones, glass, etc." Somewhat critically, one could refer to this conglomerate of bits and pieces of religious experience. More importantly, one can ask the question: How can Moravians, Scottish Presbyterians, and English Methodists be grouped under the title, "The Mosaic of Augustana's Swedish Lutheran Origins," since these three entities are neither Swedish nor Lutheran? This title is, however, appropriate because each of these influences made its mark on Swedish Lutheran life, not directly, but through the crucible of the Lutheran faith. Certain prominent Swedish Lutheran leaders were influenced by one or more of these non-Lutheran expressions of Christian experience.

Carl Olof Rosenius (1816-1868)

Carl Olof Rosenius was born in the parsonage at Nysätra in the northern province of Västerbotten. From early childhood he was sensitive to the fervent and sometimes radical pietism that often characterized the Norrland region during the nineteenth century. As a student at Uppsala, he felt that the religious atmosphere of the university lacked the warmth he had known at home; such a warmth he found, however, in Scott. As represented by Scott, the Methodist approach with its exhortation to repent of sin, to believe in Jesus Christ, and to be sanctified toward the life of the spirit, readily

11

appealed to Rosenius.

Another quality of Methodism was to mark Rosenius' ministry: the ecumenical spirit of the Methodist Church, which had its origins in the well-known statement of the founder of the denomination, John Wesley:

> One condition, and only one is required—a real desire to save the soul. Where this is, it is enough; [Methodists] desire no more; they lay stress upon nothing else; they only ask: 'Is thy heart herein as my heart? If it be, give me thy hand.'[6]

This statement of John Wesley suggests Methodism's emphasis on the emotional component of religious experience. Scott was imbued with a similar spirit. He did not attempt to convert his Swedish audiences to the Methodist point of view. "He simply urged upon his hearers the necessity of repentance for sin, faith in Jesus Christ as Savior, and a thoroughgoing amendment of life."[7] This approach strongly appealed to the spirit of the religious revival then being felt in Sweden. All the same, theologically, Rosenius was orthodox in doctrine and evangelical in spirit. He was ascetic, introspective, and tended toward belief in special religious or conversion experience as a part of Christian life.

This general view of Rosenius characterizes him inadequately. With regard to Swedish pietism, he became the leader of a trend that historians refer to as the new evangelism; some have gone so far as to call it hyper-evangelism. His emphasis differed from the so-called old pietism, which tended toward a strict application of the law. He saw God as the gentle and all-forgiving Father rather than the omnipotent divine judge of sinners. Moreover, for Rosenius, the requirement of a strong ethical life was inescapable. This, of course, was also the emphasis of the Methodists, who have been described as those who spread scriptural holiness. Finally, Rosenius' central theme was the one ·that he had learned from Luther: Humanity's salvation is through God's grace alone by faith alone. A new direction in contrast with the old pietism was well expressed by Rosenius himself in his view of the relation between law and gospel: "That which chastises sin is the law, even when it speaks through the wounds of Christ."[8]

Rosenius' own status as a layman together with his irenic nature and child-like piety did much to encourage the importance of the laity. Lay men and women now dared to take responsibility for their

Christian duties in ways that had not been the practice of the State Church of Sweden.

Rosenius not only brought to bear his influence by his preaching throughout Sweden; he was also the editor of *Pietisten* (The Pietist), a monthly newspaper that had a circulation of 10,000 in 1861. This publication was read widely not only in Sweden but also on these shores in many Augustana homes. T. N. Hasselquist, editor of the Augustana Synod's first newspaper *Det Rätta Hemlandet*, published in these pages articles that he borrowed from *Pietisten*. From 1834 to 1853, Rosenius also was responsible for *Missions-Tidning*. Very likely this newspaper had an influence on the developing interest in missions in nineteenth-century Sweden, an interest that would also become a unique part of the Augustana mosaic.

Strong as the imprint of Methodism via Scott was on his spiritual life, Rosenius did not become a Methodist. Of him it could be said as it was of Wesley, that he only cared about what one's heart religion was for Christian fellowship. Rosenius' different orientation was shown in 1856 with the organization of *Evangeliska Fosterlandsstiftelsen*. One of the factors that led to the emergence of this group, was the inability of Swedish Lutherans to continue to participate in the Evangelical Alliance. The latter had been organized in 1846 for the purpose of achieving Christian unity. When Baptists began to use this agency to propagate their own faith, however, the Swedish *läsare* (readers [of the Bible]), who constituted most of the Alliance's Swedish membership, saw the need for a confessionally committed organization. Rosenius was in the forefront of this group and together with Lundborg, he became a key figure in the founding of *Evangeliska Fosterlandsstiftelsen*. Its loyalty to Lutheran confessions is asserted in the history recorded fifty years after its inception: "To the Swedish people [*Evangeliska Fosterlandsstiftelsen*] has always carried forth the Gospel of the Cross in agreement with our Lutheran confessions."[9]

This loyalty to the Lutheran confessions, especially the Augsburg Confession and Luther's Small Catechism, characterized not only Rosenius but also those leaders from Sweden who organized the Augustana Synod. This fidelity to Lutheran confessions left its imprint on the Augustana mosaic.

Peter Fjellstedt (1802-1881)

Peter Fjellstedt's relationship with the Moravians began early in

13

his life. Forced by poverty to work in order to pay for his education, he at the age of 23 in 1826 taught at a Moravian school in Gothenburg. He did this for a year and was much attracted to these conciliatory people, especially to the head of the school, Efraim Stare. He later wrote: "I learned better to understand my inner condition of ruin and received a clear, evangelical perception of the great biblical truths."[10] Fjellstedt was also impressed by the Moravians' adherence to the Augsburg Confession. Consequently on 13 November 1826 he became a member of the Society of the Moravian Brethren. Some years later, because of a close friend's disenchantment with his own Moravian affiliation, Fjellstedt also ended his formal relationship. Nevertheless, in the subsequent years he made frequent visits to his Moravian friends in Gothenburg.

Peter Fjellstedt. From portrait, pained in Stuttga.t 1835 by Holder.
In Baron J. Hermelin's collection, Gripenberg.

14

Apart from his own testimony that the Moravians helped to clarify his own religious faith, they most certainly must have been an important factor in the development of Fjellstedt's interest in missions. So intense was this interest that he has been called the "Father of Modern Missions" in Sweden.

Fjellstedt's contributions to the Augustana mosaic were far-reaching and diverse. Best known is the institution at Lund that later moved for a brief period to Stockholm and then to Uppsala where, under the name of the Fjellstedt School, it continued for over 100 years before it closed its doors in the early 1980s. No less than twenty-six men from the Fjellstedt School completed their education at Augustana College and Theological Seminary and were ordained as ministers in the Augustana Lutheran Church. Two others, Olof Olsson and Gustaf Peters, were educated at the Fjellstedt School, the Ahlborg Catechetical School, and Uppsala University and then served as pastors in Augustana. Anders Olof Bersell, who attended the Fjellstedt School but was not ordained, served ably and faithfully as professor of French, German, Greek, and Latin at Augustana College. These men were noted for their faithful ministry; many became able leaders. In 1940, one year after of the deaths of Sven Gustaf Öhman and Sven Gustaf Youngert, Gustav Andreen, then president emeritus of Augustana College, wrote:

> As a synod we owe a great debt of gratitude to this school in Upsala [sic] for the blessed work which has gone forth both for the Swedish Church at large and for the spiritual power it sent to the Augustana Synod when it had a crying need and workers were few. . . . Thanks be to God for Fjellstedt and the Fjellstedt School for the blessings which in the past have flowed to us.[11]

A second area of Fjellstedt's impact was in the recruitment of Swedish pastors for service in America. With Lars Paul Esbjörn he shared his intense concern for missions, and we may assume that the former's interest in mission activity was thereby greatly strengthened. The influence on T. N. Hasselquist appears to have been less direct; but after Hasselquist took up his responsibilities in America, it was to Fjellstedt that he appealed again and again for financial and theological support as well as for the recruitment of men to come to America in order to serve as pastors in Augustana. Erland Carlsson immigrated to America because of the efforts of Fjellstedt, as did

Jonas Swensson. Not only did O. C. T. Andrén come to Augustana to serve as pastor in Moline, Illinois, because of Fjellstedt, but through his preaching Fjellstedt had much to do with a deepening of Andrén's spiritual life and sense of vocation. Perhaps no person was so influenced by Fjellstedt as was Olof Olsson, who was enabled to attend the Fjellstedt School because of what was seen as his great promise. Under Fjellstedt's guidance, Olsson was moved to dedicate his life to missions. Years later he called his mentor "my unforgettable spiritual father, Dr. P. Fjellstedt."[12]

Other names could be mentioned. The significance of this list is that all of these men became the leaders who were to shape the mosaic that was Augustana. Each of them made his own unique contribution, and thereby the influence of Fjellstedt can be perceived.

Fjellstedt was, moreover, a prolific writer. In 1854, he demonstrated his loyalty to the Lutheran confessions by his translation of the *Book of Concord (Evangelisk lutherska kyrkans symboliska böcker)*. This work became the standard one for several decades in Sweden. He had earlier translated Luther's Catechism, the first work that Hasselquist published with the printing press he had obtained from New York. Fjellstedt's translation of the Catechism was used in Augustana during its beginnings. On the shelves of many Augustana pastors was the three-volume commentary on the Old and New Testaments written by Fjellstedt, *Biblia det är all den Heliga Skrift, med förklaring* (The Bible: The complete Holy Scriptures with commentary).

Fjellstedt was also a journalist. He published at least four periodicals, two of which he produced for more than two decades, *Lunds Missions-Tidning* (Lund's mission newspaper) and *Bibelvännen* (The friend of the Bible). These publications were widely read not only in Sweden but also in America. The combined circulation of these two newspapers ranged from 14,000 to 20,000 and in Sweden was exceeded in popularity only by the Stockholm *Aftonbladet* (Evening newspaper). Indeed, Fjellstedt's journalistic influence was as great as was that of Rosenius.

Theologically, Fjellstedt was a moderate confessional Lutheran. "In his preaching, he stood between rigid Lutheran orthodoxy and the ecstatic fanatics. He did not find easy fellowship with strict orthodoxy. . . . Neither did he find identification with ecstatic preachers."[13] His moderate position allowed him the freedom to participate actively in a religious revival as a traveling preacher, to support the work of colporteurs, and to advocate an independent church in Sweden similar to the model furnished by the Free Church of

16

Scotland. At the same time, he was sufficiently conservative that for the most part he avoided conflict with the State Church of Sweden.

Although he wrote on every major doctrine of the Christian faith in light of Scripture and the Lutheran confessions, it was his view of the Church and the ministry that would exert the greatest impact on the Augustana mosaic. Fjellstedt saw the Church in light of the seventh article of the Augsburg Confession, which states that "one holy Christian Church will be and remain forever" and that the Church "is the assembly of all believers among whom the Gospel is preached in its purity and the holy sacraments are administered according to the Gospel."[14] Fjellstedt saw the Church as the priesthood of believers but different from the office of the ministry, even though those who occupied that office came from among the priesthood of believers. In his doctoral dissertation, he articulated his understanding of the ministry. On a basis of the Old Testament priesthood and the order of offices in the New Testament with special reference to Ephesians 4:11-16, he reasoned that God has ordained a separate order to serve the congregation. He referred to Johann Albrecht Bengel and stated that "the office is not the product of the congregation." Neither was this arrangement temporary but "should continue in the Church as an institution through which Christ for all time would be present and work in His Church."[15] Both components of the Church, as the priesthood of believers and the office of the ministry, are God's gifts: the former, God's gift to the world; the latter, God's gift to the Church.

After much debate in Augustana, this view was to prevail and become part of the Synod's constitution in 1894, where the Church was defined as:

> consisting of pastors and congregations in regular connection with the same, indicating that the ministerial office, like the congregation, is divinely instituted; the office is not a mere function created by the congregation; nor is the Church the creation of the ministerial office. Neither the Church nor office have [sic] priority over the other, but together constitute the divine institution ordained by Christ.[16]

It is of no little interest that much of the theological discussion of the Commission for a New Lutheran Church has been on this very issue. It is also significant that the direction of the thinking of that body seems to be very close to what Fjellstedt taught. This is not to claim that Fjellstedt was the only person in Sweden who held to this view. Still, the importance with which his counsel was regarded gives reason to believe that he had much to do with Augustana's view of the Church and the ministry.

It is true that Fjellstedt contributed to the Augustana mosaic through his school, as recruiter of pastors and pastoral candidates, as scholar and journalist, and as theologian. Still, few of his contributions were as significant as his work to create and heighten interest in missions. It was Fjellstedt's conviction that God had called him to become a missionary. For nearly a decade he served in this ministry, first in Pallamcottah, South India (September 1831 to February 1835) and then in Asia Minor in the vicinity of the seven churches mentioned in the book of Revelation (April 1836 to July 1840). Poor health, however, ultimately forced him and his wife, Christina Schweizerbart Fjellstedt, to return to Europe.

All the same, so intense was his commitment to the propagation of the Gospel in foreign lands, that he spent the remainder of his ministry developing interest in missions. As an agent of the Basel Mission Society, he traveled throughout Switzerland, southern Germany, the Baltic states, Scotland, England, Denmark, and Norway serving its cause. In 1846, he returned to Sweden, where he further concentrated his missionary efforts. So successful were these efforts that by the end of his life he could look back on his work as the founder of the first missionary society in Sweden, *Svenska Missions-Sällskapet i Göteborg* (the Swedish Missionary Society in Gothenburg, 1829), the first missionary institute in Lund (1846), as well as the influence of the newspaper *Lunds Missions-Tidning*, all of which significantly raised Swedish interest in the work of missions.

The dynamic of his personality and commitment also nourished the missionary interests of the pioneer leaders who shaped Augustana. Oscar N. Olson has commented: "It is largely due to [Fjellstedt's] influence that interest in missions has existed in the Augustana Church from its very beginning."[17] George F. Hall in his recent book *The Missionary Spirit in the Augustana Church* reminds us that even before Augustana was formally organized, Hasselquist as early as 1856 gave a prominent place to missions in *Det Rätta Hemlandet*. At its first annual meeting in June 1861 just one year after its establishment, Augustana formed a committee consisting of pastors Erland Carlsson, Eric Norelius, and Jonas Swensson to promote missions. Despite the limited means of these first congregations, this committee was able to report two years later that it had received $476.26 for the cause of missions. Such were the beginnings of a continuing feature of Augustana's mosaic, which had its origins in Sweden.

Lastly, Fjellstedt showed a decided interest in ecumenicism, which has also been a part of the mosaic of Augustana. As is so often the case, it may well have been that this characteristic was enhanced by his experiences as a missionary. When he and his wife embarked on this phase of their careers in 1831, there was insufficient interest in Sweden for the financial support of the young couple. Consequently, the Fjellstedts initially served under the sponsorship of the Church Missionary Society of the Anglican Church of England. The generosity of this society was indeed impressive, for even after Fjellstedt could no longer actively work in its ranks, it continued to give him a stipend for his contributions to a heightened interest in world missions. The Basel Mission Society may have been located in Reformed territory, but it was ecumenical in spirit. Lutherans were not required to lay aside their confessions in order to serve its cause. To Fjellstedt's mind, its foremost positive trait was its warm evangelical atmosphere. For the rest of his days, he referred to Basel as "the home of [my] heart."[18]

Fjellstedt was also active in the Evangelical Alliance, which had as its objective the unification of all Protestants on a nonsectarian basis, those "who with a living conviction confess their common faith in our Saviour, Father, Son and Holy Spirit, live in brotherly love and with their lives and deeds glorify that Saviour who has bought them with his blood."[19] Baptist-Lutheran conflicts in the Alliance—and the organization of *Evangeliska Fosterlandsstiftelsen* in 1856—did, of course, lessen Fjellstedt's commitment to its activities. Even so, he continued to be on friendly terms with it.

Fjellstedt's ecumenicism may well have had an influence, at least indirectly, on the ecumenical disposition that has been a prominent element in Augustana's mosaic. The leadership of the Augustana Lutheran Church in this sphere, including its early entry into both the National and World Council of Churches, is testimony to its ecumenical character.

There has been a general opinion that the chief Swedish influence in the shaping of Augustana came from Rosenius. Expressing this view is Oscar N. Olson's pronouncement: "it is safe to say that no one influenced the pioneer pastors and the early immigrants more profoundly than did Rosenius."[20] A closer acquaintance with Fjellstedt's many-sided and substantive contributions to Augustana's mosaic casts doubt on this assertion. Conrad Bergendoff more correctly assessed the situation, I believe, when he wrote: "More than ever I am convinced that [Fjellstedt's] influence on Augustana's formative years was of prime importance. Rosenius had left his mark on the laity, but I think Fjellstedt affected the ministry in a more substantive way." More specifically, Bergendoff went on to say, "Again contrasting Rosenius and Fjellstedt: while the former nourished piety, the latter was willing to tackle hard intellectual problems. The one helped form Bible school; the latter, college and seminary."[21]

Henric Schartau (1757-1825)

A third important figure in the shaping of Augustana's mosaic was the *skånske* (Scandian) clergyman and religious mentor Henric Schartau. In my estimation, we need to be reminded of his significance. His more rational viewpoint may well have served as a counterbalance to the emotional and subjective orientation of Rosenius. Like Fjellstedt, Schartau was influenced by the Moravians. Unlike Fjellstedt, however, who remained friendly to them throughout his life, Schartau reacted sharply to their Christian emphasis after his initial favorable response. He perceived them to have a subjective view of salvation, to be sentimental, and to have tendencies toward antinomianism and separatism. He also objected to their private celebration of the Eucharist.

In contrast with Rosenius and the new evangelism, Schartau was an orthodox Lutheran who placed greater emphasis on the law. Schartau felt that Rosenius' statement, "That which chastises sin is the law, even when it speaks through the wounds of Christ," gave too small a role to the place of the law in Christian experience. G. Everett Arden has observed:

> It seemed to Rosenius that God's visitation to the human heart and soul is most often experienced as a compassionate and gracious knocking at the door of the heart with an offer of pardon and peace, rather than in terms of a thunderous crash of threats and condemnation.[22]

This Schartau rejected. He was also in disagreement with Rosenius' view that God really does not require a great consciousness of sin, "just enough so that [one] can no longer live without Christ, or find peace apart from Him." To Schartau's perception, this placed too much emphasis on divine love and at the same time neglected divine wrath. Schartau believed that the new evangelism was inadequate for Christian preaching and teaching.

Schartau shared in the view of the older pietism with its emphasis on doctrine. It stressed the necessity of a thorough grounding in the Bible and doctrine through vigorous preaching and teaching with an intellectual appeal. He followed the way of Lutheran orthodoxy with its *ordo salutis* (order of salvation). His mentor in this regard was Anders Nohrborg (1725-1767). Schartau's order for the Christian life led from vocation to awakening to enlightenment, and on through conversion, regeneration, justification, and sanctification to renewal. "Schartau's rational and methodical road to salvation was a reaction against . . . emotionalism . . . and [it] attempted to counteract as well the non-confessional and unscriptural mood of the Enlightenment."[23]

"Schartau was a *churchman*, as loyal to the Church of Christ as any man that ever lived, a reformer *within* the Church."[24] He set his theology solidly in the Lutheran confessions, and the Church was the center from which Christian life, preaching, and teaching should emanate. "He willed to dwell within the Church and not erect a little church tent for his followers."[25] Schartau left the stamp of his genius in southern and western Sweden, where it is still felt. The impact of his ministry went forth from Lund, where in 1785 he began a forty-year career of preaching and teaching. He wrote a Catechism. His Friday presentations attracted crowds that filled the cathedral church in Lund.

A number of pastors in the Augustana Synod were Schartauan. S. G. Hägglund wrote an article that appeared in the *Augustana Quarterly* in December 1928, in which he noted that according to the church records of 1873 of the eighty-three pastors in Augustana, close to one-third (twenty-six) had come from Schartauan parts of Sweden. In 1927, Hägglund noted that of 822 pastors, "181 [were] clearly from Schartauan provinces . . . twenty-two percent of the Augustana clergy."[26]

Frequently during Augustana's history, it was thought that a different spirit characterized the New England and New York conferences from those of the Midwest, especially the Minnesota, Nebraska, Kansas, and Iowa conferences; the latter, it appears, were more Rosenian in their orientations. The eastern conferences were often regarded as more churchly with less stress placed on the subjective element in Christian life. Some of the most capable leaders of Augustana in the East were Schartauan, e.g., the layman Dr. Gustaf

Stolpe and his pastor son Dr. Mauritz Stolpe. The able S. G. Hägg-lund was also of this school. May not the unique spirit of the eastern region of Augustana have been significantly shaped by Schartau? This is, of course, a generalization with all of the risks that such statements entail. Still, it is a possibility that is interesting enough to deserve study so as to obtain a deeper insight into the mosaic of Augustana.

The Mosaic of Augustana

The evangelical, confessional Rosenius; the moderate, confessional Fjellstedt; the strictly orthodox, confessional Schartau: what was it that drew these three reformers together in America in a manner that did not occur in Sweden?

One of the answers to this question may be a matter of personali-ties. Hägglund has written: "Dr. T. N. Hasselquist came from Skåne, and he was probably as much of a real Schartauan as any man the Synod ever had. Nor has anyone exerted a greater influence on the making of the Augustana Synod."[27] There is little to debate in the second part of this statement. As first president of the Church and for nearly three decades president and theological professor of its college and seminary, Hasselquist wielded a strong influence. It is with the first part of Hägglund's statement that one may differ. There seems little to doubt that Hasselquist was influenced by Schartau, but he was also active, as has been pointed out, with the group that sought to model the Church in Sweden after that of the Free Church of Scotland. Also, Peter Wieselgren, temperance and revivalist leader, had a great impact on Hasselquist. Still, credence must be given to the probability that Hasselquist combined sufficiently Rosenius, Fjellstedt, and Schartau to contribute uniquely to the mosaic that became Augustana.

A more important factor, however, that brought the three together was unconditional loyalty to the Lutheran confessions. Their commitment to the Scriptures and their belief that the confessions were reliable interpretations of the Scriptures, made them of one spirit. They were united on the basic biblical tenants of the Christian faith: the triune God; human estrangement from God, both personally and corporately; the divine and human natures of Christ; and reconciliation of humanity to God through faith by grace through the crucified and risen Christ. They agreed on fundamental views

22

regarding Church, sacraments, ministry, the new life in Christ, and the final consummation of history under God's judgment as set forth in the confessions.

It was the strength of the commitment to the Lutheran confessions of Rosenius, Fjellstedt, Schartau, and others, that made Augustana an identifiable and unique community in the pluralism of American religious life. In a comparison of the Delaware Swedish Lutherans of the seventeenth and eighteenth centuries who disappeared from the American scene and the Augustana Lutherans who did not, Conrad Bergendoff has written:

> Why did these older Lutherans succumb to the environment [of Anglo-American revivalism] in Protestantism while the opponents [of Anglo-American revivalism, Swedish Lutheran immigrants] fell back on more churchly, traditional, confessional elements of their heritage? When these Augustana Lutherans broke with the 'Americanizers' were they not in line with Fjellstedt's principles?[28]

To the latter question, I would respond yes and not only to Fjellstedt's, but to Rosenius' and Schartau's, too, because upon those principles all agreed.

At an earlier point in this article, a partial definition of mosaic was given: "an inlaid work composed of bits of stone, glass, etc." Now the complete definition is in order with the addition of the following words: "forming a pattern or picture." Thus a mosaic is not a chaos of bits and pieces but an ordered or patterned arrangement of a variety of parts. Behind this pattern is a force or a principle that creates a harmony and an order that gives beauty and meaning to the whole. For the mosaic of Augustana, that force and that order stemmed from the Lutheran confessions, especially the unaltered Augsburg Confession and Luther's Small Catechism.

NOTES

[1] Karl A. Olsson, *By One Spirit* (Chicago, 1962), 29-30.
[2] Nils Rodén, "Skotska frikyrkans inflytande på svenskt fromhetsliv vid mitten av 1800-talet," *Kyrkohistorisk årsskrift* (1956): 122.
[3] G. Everett Arden, *Augustana Heritage: A History of the Augustana Lutheran Church* (Rock Island, Ill., 1963), 10-11.
[4] Conrad Bergendoff, "The Sources of the Original Constitution of the Augustana Synod 1960," *Augustana Historical Society Publications*, 5 (1935): 85; Oscar N. Olson, *The*

Augustana Lutheran Church in America 1860-1910: The Formative Period (Davenport, Iowa, 1965), 3.

[5] G. Everett Arden, *Four Northern Lights: Men Who Shaped Scandinavian Churches* (Minneapolis, 1964), 121-22.

[6] Quoted by W. W. Sweet, *The American Churches* (New York, 1948), 46-47; see also Winthrop S. Hudson, *Religion in America*, 3rd edn. (New York, 1981), 124.

[7] Arden, *Four Northern Lights*, 122.

[8] Carl Olof Rosenius, *A Faithful Guide to Peace With God* (Minneapolis, 1923, 1952), 29.

[9] Stiftelsens styrelse, *Evangeliska Fosterlandsstiftelsen. Femtionde årliga verksamhet, 1856-1906: En minnesskrift* (Stockholm, 1906), 5.

[10] Carl Anshelm, *Peter Fjellstedt, 1. Hans barndom och ungdomstid samt utländska missionsverksamhet* (Stockholm, 1930), 73.

[11] Gustav Andreen, "Sven Gustaf Youngert," *Korsbaneret*, 61 (Rock Island, Ill., 1940), 199-201.

[12] Olof Olsson, *Helsningar från fjerran. Minnen från en resa genom England och Tyskland* (Moline, Ill., 1880), 182.

[13] Emmet E. Eklund, *Peter Fjellstedt: Missionary Mentor to Three Continents* (Rock Island, Ill., 1983), 40.

[14] Theodore G. Tappert, ed. and trans., *Book of Concord* (Philadelphia, 1959), 32.

[15] Peter Fjellstedt, *Några grunddrag af nya testamentets lära om det andliga presterskapet och församlingens embeten* (Uppsala, 1857), 15.

[16] Arden, *Augustana Heritage*, 196.

[17] Oscar N. Olson, *The Augustana Lutheran Church*, 25.

[18] Anshelm, *Peter Fjellstedt*, 94.

[19] Karl A. Olsson, *By One Spirit*, 81.

[20] Oscar N. Olson, *The Augustana Lutheran Church*, 31.

[21] Conrad Bergendoff to Emmet E. Eklund, Rock Island, Ill., 8 April 1979.

[22] Arden, *Four Northern Lights*, 134.

[23] Karl A. Olsson, *By One Spirit*, 664. fn. 2.

[24] S. G. Hägglund, "Types of Piety in the Augustana Synod," *The Augustana Quarterly*, 7 (December, 1928): 337.

[25] Oscar Emil Lindberg, "Henrik Schartau. Ett hundraårsminne," *Korsbaneret*, 47 (Rock Island, Ill., 1926), 50.

[26] S. G. Hägglund, "Types of Piety," 329.

[27] S. G. Hägglund, "Types of Piety," 340. Another Schartauan in spirit, Nils Forslander, taught at the college and seminary for twenty-five years (1890-1915).

[28] Conrad Bergendoff to Emmet E. Eklund, Rock Island, Ill., 8 April 1979.

MOLDING MINISTERS TO FIT CONGREGATIONS: RELIGIOUS LEADERSHIP AMONG NEW ENGLAND'S SWEDES

Maria Erling

Late in the summer of 1899, Worcester's Swedish weekly news-paper, *Skandinavia*, began a humorous series on typical scenes in Swedish America.[1] The series ran on the first page, and on 15 August the subject was immigrant preachers. Entitled "The Last Shall be First," the story questioned whether the high status traditionally accorded to Swedish priests should be granted to immigrant preachers. The scene opened with an everyday encounter at the kitchen door: "Tall, pale, bony, his arms and legs extruding from a cheap suit—one could make no mistake about it—here was a theological seminarian." The reader followed as the student approached the back door of a prominent house on the boulevard and removed his hat with a well practiced, even stiff formality. He asked, "do any Swedish girls work here?" The paper's readers knew that it was not a vain question; Swedish women were valued domestics in many of Worcester's large houses.[2]

"Stina" who came to the door, recognized "Nils" right away; he was her old "Nesse," a former flame from the neighbor's farm. Now, to her great surprise, he was practically a pastor. "Are you studying to be a real priest!?" Straightening her apron and hair, she gasped an apology; she had been too casual in her manner. Nils averred that he was studying to be a Baptist minister. Stina stuttered an audible demotion; "Oh, a Babbetist!" But then, recalling the reason she had emigrated, she regained her poise. "After all, we are in America, and here we are all equally good." Nils went on to play on Stina's former affection; he secured financing for his ministry when he promised Stina that she might become a minister's wife.

The newspaper's humorous sketch provides modern readers with a view of the ambivalent attitudes immigrants expressed toward members of the clergy, and of their suspicions about ministers' social maneuvering. The story, by recording Stina's complex negotiation

25

between deference and familiarity, introduces us to the way that immigrants resisted older models of status and authority and by so doing changed the role that religion played in their community. Religious leaders, when slighted, created enclaves of support; these arenas of piety and deference became separate: a churchly world opposed to the wider immigrant culture.

This article will examine a key aspect of New England's Swedish culture—its religious leadership—to show that the position of minister was fundamentally altered by skeptical, reassessing immigrants, who did not accord immigrant preachers the same respect that went with the office in the old country. To be sure, there were those who expressed intense devotion to ministers, but even within deferential circles the role of pastor was transformed. Ministers no longer functioned according to the old world paradigm of a cultured and educated authority over a defined parish; instead they represented partisan factions within a larger, more fluid social world. Theological conflicts among immigrants precluded, at first, a unitary understanding of the role of religious leader; New England's industrial and urban social world, in turn, encouraged ministers to experiment with a variety of models. Preachers, after some trial and error, ultimately came to rely on the size and prestige of their congregations, rather than on credentials, social position, or theological training, to leverage respect within the larger ethnic society. A social sculpting based on leadership skills and managerial success molded the role of minister and positioned him as a representative of a bloc within the wider immigrant community. Ministers might use a variety of strategies for gaining authority within their congregations, but as they related to the immigrant community at large they came to epitomize the factional nature of New England's Swedish-American ethnic identity.

The Social Location for Swedish Ministers

Nils' path to the ministry, as reported to Stina in the story, had taken him to America, for he felt he had been endowed with a head for learning, and had bristled under the burdens of Sweden's rural poverty. Coming to America opened up, for Nils, the greatest of possibilities: he could follow God's call to ministry, and leave the cow stalls and field work behind. *Skandinavia's* account of Nils' quest lacked the respectful tone and sentimental elaboration that filled the devotional books published by church presses, but it did reflect an acquaintance with the familiar genre of immigrant spiritual biography, and especially the story line of the "call to ministry."[3] The social trajectory that Nils referred to was the same, as well. Those who heeded the call of Christ and came to America frequently travelled a path toward social advancement. Readers of *Skandinavia's* story, reminded that the past that immigrants so often wished to leave behind could come back and haunt them, were certainly amused when "Nesse's" earthly and romantic promises to "Stina" had been so clearly recalled, but they were assuredly sympathetic with the character's desire for a new start.

The newspaper's sideways questioning of ministerial ambitions was easily applied to such a marginal figure as a travelling preacher; the story, however, served also to broadcast the paper's increasing frustration with all clerical leadership. The role of minister was indeed based on the kind of back door negotiating that Nils and Stina portrayed. Among Worcester's factory workers and serving women, the deference traditionally given to Swedish priests was only partially conferred on immigrant preachers, who, like Nils, sometimes seemed to stand at the back door of the immigrant social world. Churches and ministers, promoting various hyphenated blends of Swedish-American pieties, competed with each other for influence among the devout; immigrants had to think fast when they encountered a preacher, sorting differences between Baptist and Lutheran, Mission Friend/Congregationalist and Methodist. A starting point for everyone was an image of the typical Swedish priest, but this comparison, as Stina quickly reflected, was not always an apt one.[4] Because they could not rely on a university training or the episcopal structure of the Church of Sweden to establish legitimacy—relieved, perhaps, considering the resistance among workers to that establishment—immigrant pastors in New England had to muster authority within their community and reinterpret for themselves, for their congregations, and for the public they hoped to convert, what it meant to be a minister in such a contentious setting.

The Swedish Baptists, like Nils, represented one style of religious leadership, but other religious groups within New England's Swedish communities had other models. Pastors in the Augustana Synod, which stood closest to the Swedish Lutheran tradition of an educated and highly trained ministry, struggled the hardest to bridge the distance between the back door preacher and a preferred image of the minister at the center of immigrant society. Mission Friend preachers, however, joined Swedish Methodists and Baptists to confront

Augustana's "establishment pretensions" directly. These preachers celebrated a more lay oriented and less formal model of ministry, which they felt was better suited to American conditions. When American Congregationalists undergirded Mission Friends and adopted them as Congregationalists, for example, the conflict over the preferred style of ministry became more than a theological, inner church, tangle. Augustana did not wield an establishment precedence in New England, but had to struggle to delineate its formal understanding of ministry over against an ostensibly more successful informal approach.

Contributing to the difficulty Augustana experienced in achieving a commanding presence in the region was the tardiness with which it addressed the area's serious lack of pastors. Augustana was at first represented largely by students, and only later placed full-fledged pastors in New England. As a result, Augustana preachers really competed on a level field with other Swedish-American preachers who, by virtue of their connections with American Methodists and Congregationalists, embodied another establishment.

A Level Preaching Field

During the crucial years of 1880–1885, when Swedish settlement took off, New England lacked a strong Lutheran pastoral presence.[5] The few pastors who came, unaccustomed to urban or factory lifestyles, sought to return to friends, family, and colleagues in the Midwest. Since pastors were hard to recruit, students became Augustana's answer to the frequent and ever more insistent requests by New Englanders for leaders.[6] When they arrived, following instructions to found churches, they assumed a complicated task. Preachers from other Swedish-American churches—Methodist, Baptist, or Congregationalist/Mission Friend—who were better funded, recognized by local American congregations, and in possession of clerical certification, presented stiff competition.

Several cities in New England seemed ripe for mission efforts by the 1880s; forays Augustana had made into the region revealed the increased immigrant population, as well as the presence of "sectarian preachers" who had to be countered. Before a full-time pastor could be sent to a city, however, a congregation—having the funds and authorization to issue a "call"—had to be organized. Augustana sent seminary students to the region to do this. Their reports to the Rev.

Tufve N. Hasselquist reveal how many practical hurdles had to be overcome before Augustana could enjoy the kind of presence and stature it had in the Midwest.[7] The chief difficulty that they reported, affecting ministerial credibility and congregational viability at once, was competition from free church preachers.

Augustana's students became a ready target for free church proponents who realized that these preachers could not command the stature of fully ordained ministers. Augustana students who were sent to New England also happened to share an uncertainty about their vocational plans; when they entered unchurched towns and faced competition their confusion about a ministerial career usually increased. Lacking the confidence of their rivals, these students approached leadership warily, unsure whether or not they had the stature a religious leader was supposed to enjoy. Thus the choices these students made as they shaped a particular Lutheran presence within New England's Swedish settlements—whether to emphasize their theological training or instead, to invoke their personal sense of call—were always made in opposition to the particular preaching of a rival faction. The experience of two students, both of whom later became leaders in the Augustana Synod, sheds light on the way ministers found their place in New England's Swedish community.

Ludwig Holmes came to New Britain, Connecticut, in 1883 while he was on an extended break from his studies in Rock Island.[8] He wrote to his mentor, "Uncle" Hasselquist to inform him that, even though his name had been submitted for ordination, he had firmly refused. "My head has truly not healed, and I do not have any hope that I could take up my studies. The road to the priesthood goes more and more out of my thoughts . . . but I hope to follow God's will even as I draw away from the work." To make the distance he felt from a pastoral vocation more concrete, Holmes resigned his temporary post.

Student Holmes realized that he had to give some reason for his abrupt decision to resign; he listed two factors that had soured his relationship with the congregation. First, he could not abide the fact that church members, in the absence of the regularly called pastor, were "drawn to him;" when he resisted them he felt that he was constantly "working against himself." He felt uncomfortable in New Britain, and realized that there would be rumors, but supposed that everything would settle out when he left and people could get used to their "*own* teacher." Second, Holmes mentioned a more telling reason for the tensions in the parish. People on the congregation's steering committee, he observed, were "very insolent"—they accused him of "autocratically" dismissing a decision made by the women's sewing society regarding their money. Holmes' colleague from Philadelphia, the Rev. Mr. Carl Petri, also had witnessed the "effrontery" of these people and avowed that he had been "shocked by their brutality." Holmes was uncomfortable, on the one hand, with those who came too close to him; he seemed even more offended by those who presumed, by confronting him, to level the distance further.

Holmes was no stranger to congregational tension. During the previous fall, he had agreed to preach to some Swedes in Hartford, but his work with them had undermined a Danish pastor who was trying to create a viable Danish-Swedish congregation. In New Britain Holmes encountered a church riven by social factions and gender tensions. An early history of that congregation noted how this had inhibited its growth. Some members, one writer explained, exhibited "poor breeding" and "jealousy."[9] Vague references such as these hint at the social tensions that complicated Holmes' leadership and prompted his departure. Holmes recognized that as a student he could not restore ecclesial order, or fully exercise ministerial authority. Only the regularly called pastor could do that. "Yes," Holmes concluded, "our congregations in the East are not like those in the West. They are built on loose soil and are for the most part new . . . one needs the wisdom of Solomon and the patience of Job." Holmes left New Britain for Portland, Connecticut, an older settlement, where the Swedish congregation had "churchly" members. Even though he felt that this was also a "difficult" place, he hoped it might provide a more reassuring environment.

Augustana ministers and students who came to New England longed to create and serve what they called "churchly" congregations, but few settings provided even the raw material for such a construction. Portland was one of only six places in New England that could support a Lutheran minister. The members were "rather churchly" according to one minister who worked with them. He felt that the services were well attended, and that members had worked extremely hard to build their "little church." At least, in Portland, influxes of new immigrants could be invited to God's house.[10]

Portland's "churchly" hospitality struck one newcomer who wrote home to describe the town: "There are 1,000 Swedes in Portland and we even have a Swedish church and priest as well as schools so that everything in respect of churchly relationships occurs according to

Swedish custom and practice." Immediately, however, he qualified his remarks, indicating that Portland's churchliness was somewhat fragmented: "But it is also like Sweden in that people have different views about doctrine. Some are Waldenströmian and they have a congregation for themselves. And some are Baptists . . . ."[11] Immigrants may have been reminded of home when they experienced doctrinal diversity; Lutheran preachers, however, and especially students who worked in the newest settlements, experienced "different views about doctrine" as a deeply troubling challenge. In New England, Augustana Lutherans could not rely on buildings, a university training, nor on an assured social position or salary to differentiate themselves from preachers with alternative views. Lutherans, lacking the social advantage they enjoyed in Sweden, had to muster consensus around the Lutheran confessions and their denomination's constitution with their theological training and persuasive skills.

Augustana students and ministers were distressed to find that New England's Swedes often failed to recognize their theological authority and that many seemed indifferent to doctrinal distinctions. In fact, an overweening focus on defending orthodoxy could prove to be a risky course to take. Theological acumen did not deliver congregational unity or ministerial clout in Worcester, Massachusetts, New England's largest Swedish settlement. Constantinus Magnus Esbjorn tried to steer Worcester's Lutheran Society into the Augustana Synod, but discovered that Worcester residents found his competitor's credentials and contacts with Americans more compelling.[12] The Rev. George Wiberg founded a Swedish Congregational Church, while Esbjorn scrambled to assemble the remnant of the society into a Lutheran congregation. Those thirty immigrants were mostly new arrivals; Worcester's more prominent Swedes would not support it, preferring, apparently, to wait until the disputes had subsided, or at least until Esbjorn had gone back to school. Esbjorn's defense of orthodoxy may have seemed to them but one more step toward religious and social confusion.[13]

Despite the fact that theological debate seemed counterproductive, Esbjorn was driven to a more intense engagement with theological study. His experience in Worcester made him dubious about the wisdom of grounding the authority of the minister on the subjective and malleable popular feeling in a congregation; more particularly he wondered whether the pietistic convention of the "inner call," which seemed to be a core element in his opponent's claim for authority, could provide a reliable basis for ministerial credibility. Esbjorn's experience made him wary about the procedures Augustana used to examine and approve candidates for ordination. When applied to himself, he felt that he could not relate an experience of the "inner call"; when applied to others, he doubted whether such relations were reliable. He felt, in fact, that pious rhetoric about God's call could easily be manipulated toward selfish ends. Gently prodding his mentor, Mr. Hasselquist, Esbjorn wrote: "Uncle would do me a great service, if he could make clear to me what the inner call is." Pushing further, he confessed that he resisted taking a parish call as the expedient way to be ordained, for he would have to feign an experience he had not had: "Would that be an honorable course for me to take? It has happened before in our Synod, but how have these men been perceived? God help me, [a] poor child."[14] Esbjorn desired leadership and the respect of his colleagues, but the summer's experience in Worcester unsettled him. He knew he was right about doctrine, about orthodoxy, but he was torn; he lacked the confirmation of the "inner call," and he began to wonder.

Observant students like Constantinus Esbjorn knew that there was more to ministerial leadership than the process of certification. A minister's authority, once he had completed his education and been ordained, depended on a positive relationship with a congregation. Church members confirmed their pastor's inner sense of vocation when they issued a "call;" they promised to accept and support him by paying his salary. Of course this did not guarantee that the relationship would be smooth, for pastors had to manage an often fickle and emotional relationship with congregants and at the same time gather new members. The emergence of rival congregations, however, made it easier for Esbjorn and other students from Augustana to pursue their own ideal for ministry. Those congregants that were opposed to formal ecclesial style had somewhere else to go. Competition with Mission Friend preachers led Esbjorn, and other Augustana students in New England, to a definition of ministry according to the structured, traditional, and formal aspects of the church; they grew less sympathetic to the revival.

Another shift occurred, as well, when ministers began to see "churchliness" as a function of ministerial practice and bearing, independent of parishioner deference. Augustana, through students like Esbjorn, began in New England to claim the notion of "churchliness" as a description for their unique position vis-à-vis the revival inspired free churches. They also began to differentiate themselves from the more pronounced pietism that had characterized Midwestern Augustana Lutherans.

Contrasting Ministerial Profiles

As lines between Augustana and Mission Friend preachers began to harden, and as the students who were stiffened into formalism were ordained, immigrants began to see differences in pastoral styles. Augustana students and clergymen represented the formal Swedish tradition of an educated ministry, while preachers like Carl Holm and George Wiberg championed instead their personal sense of a "call."[15] Other more tangible differences could be discerned in the various approaches to worship life. Mission and other free church preachers cultivated an informal and personal spirituality based on conversion and a pious lifestyle, while Augustana pastors carried Swedish hymnals and dressed in clerical vestments, projecting a more "churchly" formalism.

Augustana ministers visibly summoned the authority of the Church of Sweden by wearing the traditional black clerical coat with white neck tabs and leading traditional Swedish liturgies. When Lutheran ministers performed baptisms, marriages and funerals for immigrants, irrespective of their membership in congregations, they continued the inclusive practices of the old Swedish establishment.[16] Augustana pastors reminded immigrants of Swedish priests most decidedly when they took charge of the church certificates that immigrants brought with them from Sweden. New England's Lutheran congregations accepted the certificates as records of church membership—the information recorded on each form was copied onto the ledgers of huge leather bound church books. Compiling births, baptisms, confirmations, marriage and emigration dates, Lutheran pastors kept the records of the immigrant community.[17]

While pastors of Mission Friend, Methodist, and Baptist churches kept sparser books, they focused on more dramatic ways to appeal to immigrants. Expecting that membership depended on a revival, and recognizing that the gift of inspired preaching did not grace every minister, they devised a popular way to prompt the spirit. Visiting church leaders sometimes provided a reason for gathering a special crowd; more often the call went out for preachers to gather. The two- to three-day preaching festival was called a mission meeting. Attended by members of several churches, the event was intended both to bring about conversions and kick-start a local congregation, which by hosting it had the advantage of introducing a fledgling fellowship to the sage wisdom of more experienced churches. Mission meetings featured general discussion sessions alternated with rounds of preaching, worship, and fellowship. The discussion moments provided the kind of focus that kept Mission Friend pastors attuned to their audience.[18]

The friendly and consoling spiritual joy that Mission Friends sought in their fellowships did not have to be discussed at the meetings, but the kind of preaching that was needed to build a church almost always did. Mission Friends responded to a style characterized by spontaneity, fervor, and artlessness; this seemed to demonstrate a direct spiritual inspiration. Their pastors were counseled to avoid "lofty, theologically loaded" sermons "aimed between the head and the ceiling."[19] The Rev. Andrew G. Nelson, a pioneer Mission Friend preacher, provided a frequently emulated model for a heartfelt, sincere, emotional informality. The story of the beginning of his preaching career, which became a template for his whole ministry, circulated widely among Mission Friends. When "A. G." assembled a large crowd in his home, ostensibly to hear the Lutheran pastor, he had to fill in at the last minute. (Another version relates that Nelson never invited a Lutheran pastor; like Abraham on the mountain he assumed that God would provide.) "A. G." went into the back of the house, wept, prayed, and came out to read a portion of scripture. He prayed. After this "the Holy Ghost fell upon the congregation and a Norwegian backslider returned to God." The emotion of the preacher and the conversion of an unlikely sinner were the two indispensable elements of an authentic revival. Most hearers of the tale also knew that God's blessing and the absence of the Lutheran pastor were somehow connected.[20]

It was a Mission Friend commonplace to dismiss Lutheran ministers as stiff, formal, and officious. Lutheran stories accentuated the training and propriety of their pastors and decried pietist impostors. Augustana trusted that its formal system of education and examination would be capped by an "inner call" that would signify a genuine call to the ministry. Mission Friends also undertook to give their pastors a theological education, but they looked first for confirmation of an individual's "call" by more subjective means; emphasizing the importance of revivals and the encounter between the preached word and the local congregation. Augustana and Mission Friend pastors also took the criticism of their rivals to heart and some converged on a middle ground, but the primary emphasis, or the starting point for each style, was fundamentally opposed to the other. Augustana began with the formal, external shaping of the ministerial role while Mission Friends privileged the interior, emotional encounter. Immigrants in the pews noticed the difference when they went into each church—ministerial dress, the form of the worship service, and the content of the preaching—each symbolized the choice between a confessionally anchored church and a congregation swept up in the motion of a revival.

From Principled Opposition to Practical Convergence

Whatever they wore and however they spoke, Swedish ministers addressed a common challenge: appealing to the Swedish-American worker. Swedish immigration to New England steadily increased during the last two decades of the nineteenth century. The numbers fueled membership growth; but funding for ministry remained unsteady since the factory, quarry, and domestic jobs were mostly perceived by workers to be temporary. The pressures of setting up a household and working long hours also consumed much of their energy. Preachers experienced this footloose and tangential hold on New England's neighborhoods negatively; though they proclaimed a spirituality of detachment from earthly ties, they realized that they needed steadily employed lay people, and a decent portion of their income, in order to build churches.

Congregations often got off the ground when factory owners helped them out. This invited congregations and their ministers into a system of paternalism, whereby the factory owner, through beneficence to worker congregations, elicited their gratitude. In some ways the system was familiarly old world. The Augustana pastor in North Grosvenordale, Connecticut, was able to maneuver himself into what his biographer called "absolutist power;" he was on the school board, became a Justice of the Peace, and published his own newspaper. When he spoke to the factory owners about radical sectarians, he was able to get Mission Friend workers dismissed. A colleague who tried the same tactic in Rhode Island had little success, however, when owners learned the connections between these "sectarian" gatherings and local Congregationalists.[21] Augustana pastors usually were better advised to adopt a more tolerant approach toward "sectarians;" one similar to that taken by the mill

35

owners themselves, who were likely to grant land, funds, and even subsidize the ministerial salaries of Swedish churches, irrespective of doctrinal differences.[22]

Factories often dominated their workers' lives so much that they affected the interior governance of congregations, and thus pastoral leadership. Annual grants from the local company affected the internal dynamics of congregations, and tended to make leadership within churches mirror the hierarchy in the factory. It was typical, for instance, for immigrants who became foremen in the factory to extend their weekday oversight to their churches; whether elected as deacons or merely respected as the "leading men" of the congregation, such leaders influenced how pastors did their jobs.[23]

Workers could make independent choices when it came to religious life, and the usual range of options available to them—Swedish Methodist, Congregational, Baptist, and Lutheran, or no church —gradually erased the perception that the Augustana Lutheran church in town was "mainline" while other free churches had to be satisfied with a derivative status. The shift in self-perception among Mission Friends, for example, occurred in a piecemeal fashion, as the reality—that they were neither dissenters nor marginal players in New England's Swedish neighborhoods—began to dawn on them. Certainly some revivalists continued to rely on a rhetoric of oppression and fueled their message with accounts of Augustana "establishment" pretensions, but gradually Mission Friends and other free churches began to present themselves as churches in their own right.

Lowell's Mission Friend congregation negotiated the mental transition from side street to main street when they built their church in 1886. The congregation shared the rocky trajectory of most revival factions: after separating from the Lutheran congregation and struggling to gain a consensus on doctrinal issues, they finally found a preacher and received support from American Congregationalists.[24] The financial support in particular served to lead Mission Friends in a new direction; it prompted them to set aside an older, more contentious identity as dissenters and take on a new role as vanguards of a progressive, partnership styled Swedish-Americanism. Lowell Mission Friends, accustomed to vigorous debate, thus faced an identity struggle when they discussed whether to put a steeple on their "church." The moment of truth came when Carl Pihl, who was a foreman at the United States Cartridge Company, convinced members of their changed and enhanced status as American believers. Asking them to visualize their building, he persuaded them that no one walking the street should view their house of worship as less important than the Lutheran church. Mission Friends were Congregationalists and had come into their own in America; here they should no longer be juxtaposed to the Lutherans as chapel to church.[25]

Lay members like Carl Pihl in Lowell stood at the juncture of factory, family, and church, and perfected a kind of pious influence in these realms—his employees were church members and his family had a regular devotional life—that ministers idealized. Supervising the visit of a troubled nephew, Martin, when he came to Lowell, led Carl to write to his brother in Sweden: "We had a musical evening, read from God's word, thanked and prayed to God for guidance. . . happily no one has seen him take a drink . . . We spoke at length about his free will to go to an eternal ruin, or to turn to God and be a blessing to his dear parents."[26] Carl's effort to transform his nephew's life, through hymn singing, Bible reading, pious conversation, and prayer replicated the patterns of the revival, which located spiritual discipline in the home. Carl experienced his church as an extension of his family; as one of its leading members, he encouraged the Mission congregation to build its steeple.

The position of churches within their communities was interwoven with the web of personal relationships and family networks. Carl's support of the Mission Congregation was short lived. After a change in pastoral leadership, the congregation was torn by tensions and conflict that pitted Carl Pihl and his large extended family against the pastor. "Persecution and storm from within are much more dangerous than that which comes from outside," concluded one veteran. The tensions gave birth to the Swedish Methodist church where Carl soon assumed a leadership position. Lowell's historian also noted that the golden years for the city's Swedish Congregational Church had also passed.[27]

The desire for unity and social cohesion within immigrant settlements tended to steer church members away from theological debates and toward a focus on other, more practical matters such as lifestyle, or social relationships that members could govern themselves. Settlers in Natick, Rhode Island, even extended the growing inclination among immigrants to take matters into their own hands: They invented a lay focused, democratically inspired method to resolve a theological controversy. Baptist adherents in that town had hoped, by challenging the biblical basis for infant baptism, to prevent a Lutheran church from organizing. The Augustana pastor organizing the church could not diffuse the tensions. Unwilling to spend any

37

more time on the dispute, town residents asked both parties to submit to an "open debate." They proposed that "impartial observers" be brought in from Worcester, Massachusetts, who could determine once and for all who had the winning argument. The Augustana pastor, Gustaf Nelsenius, and an anonymous Baptist opponent obliged them. They prepared comments on a series of biblical passages and, as requested, interpreted them in light of their Greek, Hebrew, and Swedish renditions.[28]

Nelsenius' debate with the Baptists became a public event because immigrants needed an impartial process to resolve the tensions in their communities, and ministers themselves were viewed increasingly as partisan figures. Throughout the 1890s Lutheran ministers exchanged heated views in Worcester's paper with several preachers representing "Reformed" positions. Lutheran ministers defended their church polity against the Swedish Episcopalians in Providence, and challenged Methodists in Pontiac, Rhode Island.[29] By choosing to present their arguments regarding infant baptism, episcopal ordination, or temperance in the newspaper, ministers indicated how eager they were to have a broader forum for their views, and how ready they were to accept the paper's offer to provide an impartial arena. But the evenhanded and objective aura promoted by Worcester's newspaper created risks for ministers who were not on their toes. *Skandinavia's* circle of readers was filled with critics who used the paper to introduce their own grievances about ministers. Good Templars in Quincy had three week's worth of invective for a Lutheran minister who refused to announce or support their meetings; writers from Lowell chastised a minister who had visited their city when the Lutheran church was having problems; both parties made it clear that there were dynamics in congregations and local communities that pastors should be attuned to before they uttered their opinions. These respondents as much as said that pastors should keep to the narrow work of preaching and ministering to their congregations. Ministers, they felt, should not extend their authority any further.

Pastors: At Home and Contained Within Congregations

Skandinavia's principle for determining whether ministers should be challenged was clearly articulated in 1889. The statement was drafted to defend the paper's criticism of Worcester's Swedish

Methodist minister, who had violated a tacit understanding to keep quiet about the problems of Swedish immigrants.[30] Since his members had objected to the way that their pastor had been treated, the paper felt that they needed to be instructed about the proper role of ministers. "We do not criticize pastors who keep to their 'calling'. . . . But when a pastor lays aside his robe and enters the public arena—when he speaks for our whole nation—he is not a priest then, but a public man who should be treated like any lay man . . ."[31] All through the 1890s, *Skandinavia* held ministers accountable for their public words and actions, actively challenging ministers who seemed to wander outside their proper "call."

Swedish pastors in New England seemed to comply with the paper's limiting of their role to their congregational responsibilities; most of them had their hands full attending to the business of building up a congregation. The open debate that was scheduled in Natick, Rhode Island, and the occasional disputes that were aired in newspaper columns were expressions of the subterranean, volatile elements that gave ministers and churches their momentum and drive. These dynamics were best left buried and covered over lest they disrupt the calm and peaceful unity that seemed to increase membership. "Ordinarily," the paper explained, "we try not to get involved in the church relationships among our people other than to announce their meetings, festivals, and so on." This was a cautious editorial policy, one that would not only preserve the paper's reputation for "balance" but also keep the peace.

On *Skandinavia's* church page, however, where meetings and church festivals were announced, there was ample room for ministers and congregations to expound on their life together; there they could invite readers into their active churchly world. The columns announced the schedule of church services and meetings, but as churches grew, a more fully articulated parish family life began to be elaborated. Surprise parties honored the Lowell Swedish Methodist pastor's tenth wedding anniversary and his wife's birthday, youth leagues and sewing circle meetings met at Waltham's Lutheran parsonage. Within this enclosed and friendly world, full of surprises and group outings, familiarity and conviviality was the order of the day. Internal dissension or critique was muffled by the exuded sounds of celebration. When the Swedish Baptist minister in Worcester was given a dining room set, and the Lutheran pastor in New Britain was feted on his twenty-fifth wedding anniversary, the doctrinal differences that shaped these two assemblies faded into the background. Swedish churches converged on practices that made congregations feel like an extended family, united by bonds of affection. These social characteristics, more than theology or polity, came to define the inner contours of the churchly world.

As American churches, Mission Friend, Methodist, and Baptist congregations might continue to advertise their independence from Lutheran doctrine, but once these churches were established a more important characteristic than their theological position began to define them. The pietistic moralism of the free church revival, an inheritance that they actually shared with Lutherans, was brought to the center of religious discourse in the immigrant community. When American backing boosted the fortunes of Swedish Methodists, Baptists, and Mission Friends, it also turned up the volume of moralistic preaching. Since the moralism of the free church revival was also promoted by Augustana preachers—as a kind of pious competition to show that their Lutheranism was not the "dead formalism" that their opponents accused them of—there was almost a unanimous chorus against worldly pursuits.[32] Swedish ministers spoke out as one man against drinking, dancing, clubs, and theater, and they identified strict behavioral norms for the church centered world they controlled; the boundaries they identified separated members from the outside pleasure seeking world. Taking such an oppositional stance against the folkways of immigrant culture was not always so productive for ministers; indeed, tensions emerged among Swedish Americans and within their churches when preachers began to take on lodges and other secular associations. Within congregations, however, and among church people, the behavioral codes served to delineate an ideal of a religious Swedish-Americanism.

During the first decade of the 1900s Constantinus M. Esbjorn was in New Haven and Ludwig Holmes, in "dear" Portland, Connecticut. They were joined by other ministers who shared their "churchly" leanings; one of them was the Rev. Carl Bergendoff, an Augustana pastor who lived in Middletown, Connecticut. He provides a capstone to the construction of Augustana's ministerial identity in New England. He knew he had to entice immigrants, not compel them, into a religiously centered social life. His style contrasted with that of the neighboring Mission preacher; Bergendoff kept the Swedish church books in good order and emphasized a formal worship. But like all Swedish ministers in New England, Bergendoff introduced youth leagues, church choirs, a Sunday school, and a summer Swedish school to Middletown's Lutheran church. The

Rev. Carl A. Bergendoff. (Courtesy of Augustana College Library, Special Collections.)

church world that he fostered became so encompassing to Middletown's Lutherans that members could almost ignore their rival congregation down the street. Carl Bergendoff's son, Conrad, grew up in Middletown after the turn of the century and knew of the other Swedish congregation, but their separate religious life did not affect his own: "Growing up I learned that we were an immigrant community, accepted but different. The congregation was not large, but it was the center of the social interests, as well as religious. There was a small Mission congregation, and some tension between them [and us], but more indifference."[33] The world beyond the congregation that was most important to young Conrad was the Augustana Synod, and he was not alone with that feeling. Youth leagues, conference meetings, and mission events—highpoints on a church centered calendar—brought Middletown's Lutheran church into a wider network and expanded the boundaries of their churchly world.

Swedish ministers in New England identified themselves, by 1900, as leaders of a churchly world set apart from the immigrant culture around them. They did not, however, carve out this niche on their own. Partly confined to a separate stance by immigrants who resented priestly encroachment; ministers also stood aloof and constructed boundaries to protect and preserve religious practice, which provided a secure domain for the role of pastor. Tightly connected to local assemblies, pastors did more than defend theological positions or preach for revival. Congregational work became broader than preaching or teaching, *per se*, and included functions that nurtured immigrant social life. Managing a congregational family became the specialized province of immigrant pastors; they measured their status by their ability to draw in members and construct large churches. From an institutional base, ministers became representatives of separate communities and were authorized by them to venture out into a larger immigrant culture. Congregations and ministers together created an oppositional dynamic as they confronted the lifestyles and folkways of immigrant society and offered a church centered lifestyle as an alternative.

NOTES

[1] The sketch was written by Johan Person, a journalist on *Skandinavia's* staff in 1899. His literary career is discussed in Ulf Jonas Björk's essay "Making Swedish America Visible: The Fiction and Essays of Johan Person," *Swedish American Historical Quarterly* 45 (1994): 196–216.

[2] More about this occupational choice among Swedish women—one that prompted its own migration patterns—is in Inga Holmberg's contribution to *Swedish Life in American Cities*, Dag Blanck and Harald Runblom, eds., Uppsala Multiethnic Papers, 21, Uppsala University, 1991, pp. 25–43.

[3] Spiritual biographies [necrologies] of Augustana pastors and lay leaders were printed in *Korsbaneret* [The Banner of the Cross], a devotional annual published in Rock Island, Illinois, from 1883–1945. *Hemåt* [Toward Home], provided the same inspiration for Mission Friend/Covenant readers. The early issues of *Korsbaneret* contained lengthy biographies and embroidered deathbed scenes. Later, pastors grew impatient with the way that some of their colleagues were posthumously transformed; the entries became shorter and much more perfunctory. The correspondence of C. J. Bengtson, a pastor in Hartford who later edited the *Lutheran Companion*, reveals the impatience of younger, English-speaking pastors with the vaulted piety of the older generation. Evangelical Lutheran Church of America (hereafter abbreviated as ELCA) Archives, Chicago, Illinois.

[4] Swedish immigrant pastors did not enjoy (or suffer) the reputation of Swedish priests. Very few priests from the Church of Sweden emigrated. Aside from an initial trickle

of "pioneer" pastors who, though ordained in Sweden, felt they had a better future in America and came to Illinois in the 1850s and 60s, pastors who served immigrant congregations were educated in America, mostly by immigrant pastors, at church run institutions.

[5] Six cities—Boston, Worcester, and Campello, Massachusetts; Pontiac, Rhode Island; Portland and New Britain, Connecticut—had regularly–called Lutheran pastors. Each setting had Mission Friend gatherings. In Worcester, Swedish Methodists organized in 1878. In the late 1880s a pattern developed that combined doctoral study at Yale with pastoral work in Ansonia, New Britain, Hartford, New Haven, and Meriden. Conrad Bergendoff, *The Augustana Ministerium 1850–1962*, Rock Island: Augustana Historical Society, 1980, documents that Yale was more popular than the University of Chicago or Harvard. As late as 1910, Augustana's Hartford District minutes reveal the continued reliance on students. "Our district consists of twenty eight congregations, fourteen pastors, and five students."

[6] Augustana's Eastern mission director, in an early address describing the history of the New York Conference, castigated Augustana leaders for leaving immigrants to "unbelief" and "sect makers;" early ministers were also blamed—"any pastor who came to one of the eastern cities left after a short time." Gustaf Nelsenius, undated. ELCA Archives, Chicago, Illinois.

[7] The encounters of students with recalcitrant parishioners are preserved in reports to the Rev. Tufve Nilsson Hasselquist, the aging Augustana patriarch. At the end of his career, he was still involved in recruiting and guiding the formation of ministers. When students wrote to him they were very consciously shaping a pastoral identity. Their correspondence reveals, of course, only one side of the social situation.

[8] Ludwig Holmes (1858-1910, ordained 1886) became Augustana's poet laureate. Two of his pastorates were in Connecticut.

[9] The Swedish word *avundsjuka*, or resentful jealousy, was at times identified by contemporaries as a national character flaw. See *Svenskarna I Rhode Island* [Swedes in Rhode Island], Worcester: Svea, 1916. The term had high currency value in the descriptions of community life; it was often cited as the cause of tension or disunity.

[10] The pastor serving in Portland (1880–85), John Mellander, described the congregation this way in a letter to Hasselquist on 4 March 1880.

[11] August Troedsson, Portland, Conn., 15 June 1889. August worked in the stone quarries and did odd jobs for the church, digging graves at the cemetery.

[12] Constantinus Magnus Esbjorn (1858–1911, ordained 1888) became a professor at Augustana's Seminary from 1883–1900. His last parish was in New Haven, Conn.

[13] Hans Trulson, a merchant, made a revealing comment in 1889 about early church life among Worcester's Swedish settlers. Speaking of dissension among his fellow countrymen he noted: "sixteen years ago we had one church group, [at that date Swedish children were baptized at All Saints Episcopal Church] but now there is much more factionalism." He hoped a political club would bring unity. *Skandinavia*, 28 December 1889.

[14] Letter to Hasselquist, Worcester, Massachusetts, 19 August 1881. Esbjorn also reveals in this letter that his options had been narrowed by the piety of his synod once before. "I was not allowed to devote myself to humanistic studies, and now maybe I will not be allowed to be a theologian either."

[15] "No church body, to our knowledge, had higher requirements for its pastor's education." Conrad Bergendoff, *The Augustana Ministerium, 1850–1962*, Rock Island: Augustana Historical Society, 1980. p. 2.

¹⁶ Carl A. Benander's record of the pastoral acts he performed between 1887–1912 reveal that over sixty percent of the baptisms were for non–member parents. Archives of Immanuel Church, Boston, Mass., now Resurrection Lutheran Church, Roxbury, Mass.

¹⁷ Immigrants took great care of these papers; they contained the full documentation of their former citizenship. But church books were controversial in New England's settlements; Mission Friend pastors who tried to draw up membership lists heard sentiments like this: "We don't want our names to be written in any congregation book, for they are written in heaven." Paul Peter Waldenström, *Handlingar rörande Svenskarnes andliga och socialla ställning på vissa platser i Amerikas Förenta Staterna* [Handlingar] (Accounts of the spiritual and social situation among Swedes in the United States), Stockholm, 1891. pg. 70.

¹⁸ In 1897 the Eastern Ministers Association discussed: "Is it right to preach that a person can be saved no matter how low they may have sunk?" During the discussion sessions in 1900 participants seemed to wonder if friendliness had gone too far: "Should a Christian always express him or herself with friendly words, or, is one never permitted to speak harshly?"

¹⁹ The hymn writing of Swedish pietists was also influenced by this aversion to formal style. See Inger Selander, *O hur saligt att få vandra: Motiv och symboler i den frikyrkliga sången* [Hymns of the Free Churches in Sweden: Motifs and Symbols], Stockholm: Gummesons, 1980, especially ch. 1.

²⁰ A. G. Nelson died as the oldest living Covenant pastor in 1943 when he was 92. His obituary was recorded in *Our Covenant*, 1943, pp. 131–2.

²¹ *Österns Veckoblad* reported in February 1887 that the Augustana pastor in North Grosvenordale, a tiny milltown in Connecticut, had convinced the factory owner to suspend workers who attended Mission Friend meetings. The newspaper warned that old world practices had come to America via Augustana. Another Lutheran minister tried to interfere with Mission meetings in Crompton, Rhode Island, but after a Mission Friend became a foreman in the factory the persecution stopped. J. S. Österberg, *Svenskarna i Rhode Island*, Worcester: Svea Publishing Company, 1915, p. 131.

²² Congregational records in New England mill or quarry towns, Lutheran and otherwise, record the help of employers. The owner of the quarry in Proctor, Vermont, for instance, built churches for both the Mission Friends and the Lutherans. St. Paul Swedish Evangelical Church, Proctor, Vt., records. A discussion of factory paternalism informs Charles Cheape, *From Family Firm to Modern Multinational: Norton Company, A New England Enterprise.* Cambridge, Mass: Harvard University Press, 1985. The Norton Company was a strong influence on Swedish culture in Worcester.

²³ John Jeppson, a co–owner of the Norton Company, found a good working relationship with John Eckström, pastor of the largest Lutheran church in Worcester from 1905–1940. Jeppson paid half the building costs for a large gothic structure the congregation built in 1915. Norton employees were paid by the company to work on the construction, as well. In Lowell, Anton Söderberg, a foreman at a textile plant, became known as a particularly "tyrannical" deacon. His tight hold on leadership led to an effort to unseat him in 1903. The mutiny was foiled by the pastor, who repaid in this way years of favorable support.

²⁴ American funding enabled Mission Friend congregations to get on solid footing but even with money it was sometimes difficult to get preachers. In Boston theological differences had to be resolved before there was sufficient unity to attract members. Paul Peter Waldenström, [Handlingar], Stockholm, 1891. pp 102–109.

²⁵ It was the businessmen within the congregation that made this point. For them, it

seemed to be a matter of status; they did not feel that their church should appear to be any less important than the Augustana church.

[26] Carl Pihl to Axel Pihl, 30 January 1901. Pihl archives, HMA 1580, Hallands Länsmuseet in Halmstad, Sweden.

[27] Olof Berntson, *Kort Historik över Svenskarna i Lowell*, Lowell, 1917, pg. 27.

[28] J. S. Österberg, *Svenskarna i Rhode Island*, Worcester: Svea Publishing Company, 1915, p. 104.

[29] An Augustana pastor in North Grosvenordale, Göran Forsberg, started his own church newspaper and used it to counter the mission efforts of the Episcopalians.

[30] The Rev. Mr. Eklund had, in that year, made a public appeal in the local American paper for aid to indigent Swedish immigrants. Swedish leaders felt that American benevolence compromised the image they wished to present.

[31] *Skandinavia*, 4 January 1889.

[32] See Elmer Engberg, "Augustana and Code Morality," *Centennial Essays*, Oscar Benson, ed. (Rock Island: Augustana Book Concern, 1960), pp. 122–149. Constantinus Esbjorn, before he left Worcester, cast aspersions on the more ostensibly pious Mission Friends when he heard rumors about a woman in their circle. He speculated on the religious intimacy in their "pure" congregation: "What an embrace!" Esbjorn wrote, insinuating that the emotion in their revival was anything but pious. Letter to Hasselquist, 9 August 1881.

[33] Private letter to author, 26 May 1991.

CONRAD BERGENDOFF AND THE SWEDISH-AMERICAN CHURCH LANGUAGE CONTROVERSY OF THE 1920s

H. Arnold Barton

To the great majority of Swedes in America during the height of the Great Migration, it went without saying that their native language was the Lord's favored tongue. To be sure, the very earliest immigrants had not shown much sentimental attachment to their native language. But the far larger influx of Swedes from the mid-1860s onward strongly reinforced its standing in the immigrant community.[1]

The American-born Pastor Carl Aaron Swensson wrote that in his childhood "it was considered fine by many to have forgotten Swedish . . . sometimes even before they had had time to learn English." By his student years, however, he recalled a growing enthusiasm for Swedish at Augustana College and Seminary, first in Paxton and even more after the move to Rock Island, Illinois, in 1875. "We sang Swedish songs with greater fervor than before. . . . The Swedish that was spoken became more fluent, and that which was written more correct. It was a Swedish era at our synod's college."[2]

Yet Swensson's description already makes clear that correct and fluent Swedish did not come altogether easily to the children of Swedish immigrants born, or at least raised, in the new land. The Swedish journalist, Ernst Beckman, visiting the United States in 1882, was told indeed that the Swedish Americans were now more attached to their native language than formerly. Although there were still parents who did not want their children to hear Swedish at all, most learned both languages in the home. Yet he observed that among themselves the children seemed to prefer English and that "Swedish seems difficult and awkward to them." Moreover, their Swedish was a "peasant dialect, which they are ashamed of," whereas "in English they speak as properly as anyone else."[3]

The decade between 1900 and 1910, when the first- and second-generation Swedish element reached its peak in the U. S. population, represents the high water mark of *svenskhet*—Swedish language and culture—in America. "There exists in this country a new Sweden," the Augustana Lutheran pastor Lars Gustaf Abrahamson wrote proudly in *Prärieblomman* in 1903, adding rather over-optimistically, "Here there are up to two million citizens who proudly trace their origins back to Sweden; who speak their forefathers' language, read their literature, and cherish their history."[4]

To C. A. Swensson, the cultural role of the church he served was a matter of deep pride. "The Swedish Lutheran Church in America, or Augustana Synod, which is the same thing, has been the standard-bearer of the Swedish heritage among our countrymen in this land," he wrote in 1890. "The Augustana Synod," the American-born pastor L. A. Johnston proudly proclaimed in the volume commemorating its fiftieth anniversary in 1910, "has, more than anything else, upheld the spiritual and cultural relationship with the old homeland, preserved Swedish culture, advanced higher education, and above all maintained the Swedish language and the Christian heritage which Svea's children brought with them from their old fatherland."[5]

Yet as early as 1880 it was beginning to become evident that the balance between the linguistic and the religious heritage was an uneasy one at best; at the synodical meeting of that year concern was expressed over a loss of young people to other denominations, due to their preference for English. Certain congregations began to alternate English with Swedish services. In 1908 some fifteen of the Synod's churches and missions organized an Association of English Churches, joined by others in the years that followed, with the goal of preserving "the faith of the fathers in the language of the children." The non-Lutheran Swedish-American denominations meanwhile continued to hold more closely to the old language.[6]

World War I imposed a heavy ordeal upon America's immigrant groups and the survival of their languages, especially after the entry of the United States into the conflict in April 1917. Anti-foreign sentiment ran high and the Swedes, together with the Norwegians, suffered accordingly, since they had initially tended to favor Germany—the foe of Sweden's traditional arch-enemy, Russia, and the bastion of Lutheranism—and had generally opposed American intervention in the war. Rampant "100% Americanism" continued after the armistice, thanks to the Bolshevik Revolution of 1917 in Russia and resultant fears of foreign radicalism. Beginning in 1918, twenty-two states passed legislation banning or restricting the public use of foreign languages, before this was declared unconstitutional by the Supreme Court in 1920.[7]

During the war years the pressures of the Americanization campaign surely helped to persuade a few Augustana Lutheran congregations—primarily, it would seem, in older areas of settlement with a high proportion of American-born members—to go over entirely to English. The trend continued after conditions returned to normal by the early 1920s and accelerated when the immigration quota laws of 1921, 1924, and 1927 progressively reduced the flow of immigration from the Old Country.

This development was viewed with mounting alarm in Sweden, where the emigration question had become a burning issue after the turn of the century. Great efforts had been made, publicly and privately, to stem the flow. Another reaction to the crisis was meanwhile to seek to turn the large overseas Swedish population to account in promoting Sweden's wider cultural and national interests in the world. This latter ideal was espoused by the Society for the Preservation of Swedish Culture in Foreign Lands (*Riksföreningen för svenskhetens bevarande i utlandet*), established in Gothenburg in 1908, and by its dedicated chieftain, Professor Vilhelm Lundström, for whom language was the Alpha and Omega of culture.[8]

Vilhelm Lundström. (Courtesy of Riksföreningen Sverige-kontakt, Göteborg.)

48

The American wartime language restrictions provoked a strong reaction in the society's newspaper, *Allsvensk samling*, which denounced them as worse than the oppression of national minorities in imperial Russia, Germany, and Austro-Hungary. It featured numerous articles under such titles as "Language Persecution" or "Shall the Swedish Language Be Murdered," based upon reports from aroused Swedish Americans. Under such circumstances, the abandonment of Swedish by an Augustana congregation in Iowa seemed more than ever to be nothing short of rank betrayal of the common heritage. "In truth, one is wordless at such a display of cowardice and toadying to the Americans!" *Allsvensk samling*—doubtless in the voice of Vilhelm Lundström—editorialized in May 1918. "But if the Fort Dodge Swedes hope they can win the Americans' respect by so deeply debasing themselves, their nation, and their language, they are certainly mistaken." It was to be hoped nonetheless that the ordeal would separate the wheat from the chaff, the paper declared in May 1919, and "one faithful soul, who works and strives, means more than ten renegades."[9]

If anything, the continued Americanization campaign following the armistice appeared even more ominous to Lundström and the *Riksförening*: it seemed to prove that what might simply have been a wartime hysteria was in fact becoming concerted policy, a "strong, deliberate, and . . . ruthless nationalism," an "anticultural, despotic agitation for the unbridled tyranny of a dominant language."[10]

Such attacks from the old homeland called forth indignant responses from Swedish Americans, including Augustana Lutheran pastors. America must not allow itself to be weakened in its hour of crisis, wrote Pastor Carl J. Bengtson, the Swedish-born editor of the Augustana Synod's English-language *Lutheran Companion* in July 1918,

> and the sooner our friends over in Sweden learn this the better. If we cannot have relation with them on any other basis than that we retain and perpetuate every racial distinction as to language, mode of thought, and point of view and love of heart, then we are better off without retaining relation with them at all. . . . in America we neither can nor will perpetuate the things that necessarily would keep us separate from the American people.[11]

After mid-1919, *Allsvensk samling* evidently saw fit to taper off its attacks on America in the face of Swedish-American resentment, and as the Americanization campaign abated. But the respite was brief, for Vilhelm Lundström and his friends in Sweden now saw looming before them a still more insidious and fateful threat to *svenskhet* in America: its betrayal by the Swedish-American churches themselves, with the venerable Augustana Synod in the lead.

To those who strove to uphold the Swedish heritage, both in America and in the homeland, it was self-evident that language and culture were inseparable and must stand or fall together. Traditionally they regarded the Augustana Lutheran church as the bulwark of the Swedish presence in the new land. For the Synod itself to capitulate would mean nothing less than the betrayal of its sacred trust and would throw open the gates of the citadel.

Signs had not been lacking of impending peril. It was, for instance, more than wartime pressures that in December 1917 prompted Rev. Samuel Miller to write in the *Lutheran Companion*:

> Shall we go on and dream of preserving a Swedish church in America until other churches have taken all our children? Some of us who were born and brought up in this country do not at all feel that it is our duty to preserve Swedish culture and the Swedish language in America, but rather to inject all the inherited good things into the stream of American life by means of the language that America speaks and understands. ... Oh! my dear Augustana Synod, is the future worth nothing to you? Wilt thou insist on being blind to *the inevitable*?[12]

The champions of *svenskhet* were neither unaware of nor unconcerned about such rumblings, as the reaction of *Allsvensk samling* to the Fort Dodge congregation's language shift in 1918 made clear. Beginning in June 1921 the paper launched an impassioned campaign against language concessions within the Augustana Synod. Up to this point *Allsvensk samling* had criticized its clergy simply for faintheartedness in the defense of the ancestral language and culture. In June 1921 it raised a new and far more serious allegation, which it henceforward constantly reiterated: that the decline of Swedish in the church was not simply due to negligence, but rather to the deliberate policy of its leadership, despite the rising protests of its membership. Over the next three years a barrage of articles in *Allsvensk samling* came out under such titles as "How the Swedes Are Seeking to Kill the Swedish Language in America" or "How Swedish Is Being Eradicated." They repeatedly held up the Finland-Swedes as models of steadfastness in upholding *svenskhet*, both in Finland and in the United States.[13]

The Augustana clergy long bore this cross with remarkable fortitude. Most of them were still warmly attached to their Swedish language and heritage, and took great pride in all that their church had done for over six decades to cultivate them on American soil. Many were staunch members of the Society for the Preservation of Swedish Culture in America, the offspring of the Swedish *Riksförening* established in 1910. Thus, while stoutly confronting the outright Americanizers within their church, they found it all the more galling to have to face bitter accusations from the old homeland. Yet ultimately they too could not but place faith before language. As Pastor A. T. Seashore had put it already in 1908, "It is not that we love Swedish less, but that we love souls more."[14]

Ultimately the Synod's spokesmen could hardly fail to respond. The first to take up the gauntlet was the then 28-year-old, Nebraska-born Dr. Conrad Bergendoff, a graduate of Augustana College and Seminary, and of the University of Chicago, then pastor of Chicago's Salem Lutheran Church, who from 1935 to 1962 would serve as president of his alma mater in Rock Island.[15] In April 1924 he came out—in flawless and expressive Swedish—with a firm but hopefully conciliatory defense of his church in the pages of *Allsvensk samling* itself.

A misunderstanding, he wrote, had arisen in Sweden regarding Augustana's viewpoint, and he had thus far waited in vain for someone to defend it.

> The Augustana Synod's position regarding the Swedish language must be judged from a religious, not from a cultural, standpoint. The preservation of the Swedish language has never been, is not, and can never be this synod's objective. Those who criticize a church's use of one language or another should not forget that the Church exists for the sake of religion and not of culture. Language must be a means in the service of the Church. . . . A living church, like a living body, adapts to its circumstances and makes use of such means as can best serve its proper goal.

The Lutheran message, he went on to say, should be accessible not only to Swedish Americans. In this connection, he raised a sensitive issue:

51

The Church works best where she is welcome, and the latest immigrants from Sweden have not shown themselves interested in the ministrations of the Church. . . . The Augustana Synod is as Swedish as its membership is Swedish. And when she is not welcomed with gratitude by those who prefer the Swedish language, she turns, with the best precedents [i. e. the Apostle Paul's] to the 'children of the Greeks,' who only understand English.

Conrad Bergendoff, ca. 1925. (Courtesy of Augustana College Library, Special Collections.)

The Synod simply lacked the resources to teach children Swedish when their parents failed to do so. "We repeat: the Augustana Synod is Swedish where Swedes are faithful to the Church." However, "One who speaks Swedish because he cannot speak English," he cautioned, "is Swedish-minded of necessity, not through love." As its primary aim, the Synod strove to keep alive the "spirit of the Swedish church," which in itself was sufficient justification for it to maintain its independent position, even toward other Lutheran churches in America.

Augustana was naturally also interested in Swedish culture. "In all of America," he stated, "there is no organization that has so greatly honored its fatherland and mother tongue." Many in the Synod were still bilingual and showed their love for the old language. Moreover, "The younger generation is interested in the Swedish heritage when it reveals itself as a culture." "Augustana's heart is still Swedish, regardless of which tongue it may speak." But, Bergendoff warned in conclusion, zealots

> all too often exalt the Swedish heritage by belittling America's culture and spirit. Such persons have no understanding of America's history and soul, and will never win friends for Swedish culture. The tree of the Swedish heritage is known by its fruits. . . . Preservation of the Swedish heritage means for me that the Swedish spirit, and not only the tongue, should be saved. For this kind of preservation of the Swedish heritage the entire Augustana Synod strives.[16]

Bergendoff's article in *Allsvensk samling* was accompanied by no direct editorial comment, but it was followed on the same page by two communications from impassioned defenders of the mother tongue in America, Axel H. Helander in Worcester, Massachusetts, and the Augustana pastor Emil Lund in Minneapolis, the latter decrying the "*ruthless* assault upon all that is Swedish!" "May we fight," Lund urged, "for what still remains of the Swedish heritage, even with only the 'courage of desperation.'" *Allsvensk samling* thereby effectively reiterated its own unwavering stand.[17]

As this exchange of viewpoints from Swedish America made clear, the battle was far from over. Attacks in *Allsvensk samling* against Augustana's language policy continued to proliferate, and the Synod's clergy now responded in kind. In May 1924, the editors of its Swedish-language periodical, *Augustana* (L. G. Abrahamson and Carl Kraft) accused *Allsvensk samling* outright of presenting a distorted picture in Sweden of the Synod, which continued to make great efforts to preserve Swedish language and culture, but which nevertheless had to face reality. If the church did not use English among those who did not know Swedish, *Augustana* wrote in July 1924, "then, along with our congregations, our colleges and our cultural work will also go under."[18]

In an article printed in a number of Swedish newspapers, Vilhelm Lundström delivered his bitterest attack on the Synod in April 1925. "Once the will to remain Swedish has died out within the Augustana

Synod, it will have betrayed its historic mission. . . [and] every trace of Swedish tradition will soon be swept away." In his disillusionment he now wondered whether the defense of *svenskhet* in America should not instead be entrusted to the Swedish-American secular societies.[19]

Lundström was at this point beginning to place his fondest hopes in the largest of these organizations, the nationwide Vasa Order of America, founded in 1896. Already in 1924, a tour of Sweden by a group from the Vasa Order's recently organized children's clubs, who performed Swedish songs and dances in folk dress, offered him hope of regaining the older generations through the enthusiasm of the younger.[20]

To the Augustana Synod this was to add insult to injury, for although passions had cooled somewhat since the turn of the century it had long regarded the Swedish-American secular societies as dangerous rivals and still harbored a certain mistrust toward them. *Augustana* responded vigorously, in effect reiterating the standpoint set forth by Conrad Bergendoff in 1924. As for the Vasa Order, *Augustana* editorialized in December 1925, while it had sent over to Sweden "a few dozen children born in this country" the year before, "we would be able to send many thousands of children who have been born into our congregations, who understand and speak the language of their fathers." Compared with Augustana's Swedish-language activity, it proudly maintained, that of the societies paled into insignificance.[21]

Already by 1924, Pastor Emeroy Johnson complained in the *Lutheran Companion* that "this narrow-mindedness among people on both sides of the language problem constitutes a greater problem for our synod that the language problem itself." Nonetheless, after 1925 the controversy gradually died out. Older Augustana Lutherans came increasingly to accept that "the Lord can speak to their hearts even in English," as the Illinois Conference recognized in 1921. Census figures meanwhile record the ever-growing proportion of second-, as compared with first-generation Swedish Americans: already by 1930 the Swedish-born amounted to only a little over a quarter of the total enumerated Swedish stock in the United States. Even so, the transition to English proceeded only slowly over the following decades.[22]

Meanwhile, the American quota law of 1924, combined with improved living standards at home, reduced Swedish emigration to a relative trickle. Thus, in Sweden earlier patronizing or contemptuous attitudes toward the emigrants began to give way. There was a growing tendency, now that emigration no longer represented a threat to the nation's well-being, to view them in retrospect as stout-hearted pioneers who had proved what Swedes were capable of achieving out in the world. This shift in attitude was, for instance, reinforced by the enthusiastic account given by Archbishop Nathan Söderblom, the primate of the Swedish state Lutheran church, following his visit to the United States in 1923, including much praise for the Augustana Synod. It was reflected in the handsome and laudatory two-volume collaborative work, *Svenskarna i Amerika*, published in Stockholm in 1925-26, with contributions—for the first time—by both Swedish and Swedish-American writers. And it was triumphantly confirmed by the official visit to the United States of Crown Prince Gustav Adolf (later King Gustav VI Adolf) in 1926.[23]

Life went on. The *Riksförening* turned its attention by the later 1920s increasingly to the support of the Swedish-speaking minorities in Finland and Estonia, and to sponsoring Swedish lectureships at foreign universities.

But it is worth mentioning as a sequel that when Vilhelm Lundström finally visited the United States for the first and only time in 1938, two years before his death, he was surprised and gratified to find that *svenskhet* there was still far more vital and durable than he had thought possible.[24] At the end of the century, it lives on still, even if, by now, more in spirit than in tongue, as Conrad Bergendoff had foretold in 1924, when he dared to think what until then had scarcely seemed conceivable. It remains to say that Vilhelm Lundström departed the scene 55 years ago, in 1940, whereas Conrad Bergendoff is still with us. One may interpret this as symbolically as one will.

NOTES

[1] See my article, "The Life and Times of Swedish America," *Swedish-American Historical Quarterly* 35 (1984): 282-96.
[2] C. A. Swensson, *I Sverige. Minnen och bilder från mina fäders land* (Stockholm, 1891), 17-20.
[3] Ernst Beckman, *Amerikanska studier*, 2 vols. (Stockholm, 1882), I:139-42.
[4] L. G. Abrahamson, "Licentiat C. L. Sundbeck och betydelsen af hans resa i Förenta Staterna," *Prärieblomman 1903*, 101-02. On the standing of Swedish in America in this period, see my book, *A Folk Divided: Homeland Swedes and Swedish Americans, 1840-1940* (Carbondale, Ill., 1994), 219-22. According to the U. S. Census Bureau, the Swedish element in 1910 numbered around 665,000 Swedish-born plus nearly 700,000 persons

born in the U. S. of Swedish-born parents, for a total of 1,363,554. Cf. Sture Lindmark, *Swedish America 1914-1932* (Uppsala and Chicago, 1971), 11-12.

[5] Swensson, *I Sverige*, 17; *Minneskrift med anledning af Augustana-Synodens femtioåriga tillvaro* (Rock Island, Ill., 1910), 477-78.

[6] Lindmark, *Swedish America*, 210, 260-64; Nils Hasselmo, *Amerikasvenska. En bok om språkutveckling i Svensk-Amerika* (Stockholm, 1974), 55-57. For a general discussion of the church language controversy, see, besides the above, George M. Stephenson, *The Religious Aspects of Swedish Immigration* (Minneapolis, 1932), chs. 20-30; my *Folk Divided*, chs. 15-17.

[7] See Lindmark, *Swedish America*, ch. 6; my *Folk Divided*, 245-50. Cf. Carl H. Chrislock, *Ethnicity Challenged: The Upper Midwest Norwegian-American Experience in World War I* (Northfield, Minn., 1981).

[8] On Lundström and the *Riksförening*, see Bengt Bogärde, *Vilhelm Lundström och svenskheten* (Göteborg, 1992) and my review of this book, in *Swedish-American Historical Quarterly* 44 (1993): 166-68; my *Folk Divided*, 267-68.

[9] *Allsvensk samling* (Göteborg, 1922), esp. 1 May 1918, 3; 1 March 1919, 3-4; 1 May 1919, 2-3. Cf. my *Folk Divided*, 267-68.

[10] *Allsvensk samling*, 2 January 1919, 1-2.

[11] *Lutheran Companion*, 20 July 1918, 368.

[12] *Lutheran Companion*, 22 December 1917, 639-40. Cf. ibid., 31 March 1917, 151.

[13] *Allsvensk samling*, esp. 15 January 1921, 4; 1 June 1921, 3; 15 August 1921, 3; 15 February 1922, 3; 1 December 1922, 5-6; 15 February 1923, 4; 16 April 1923, 5; 3 May 1923, 3; 15 June 1923, 2; 1 March 1924, 3; 1 April 1924, 2; 15 May 1924, 4-5, 6.

[14] Lindmark, *Swedish America*, 264.

[15] Conrad Bergendoff, *The Augustana Ministerium, 1850-1962* (Rock Island, Ill., 1980), 107.

[16] Conrad Bergendoff, "Augustana-Synoden och svenskhetens bevarande," *Allsvensk samling*, 15 April 1924, 3.

[17] *Allsvensk samling*, 15 April 1924, 3-4.

[18] *Augustana*, 1 May 1924, 280-81; 2 July 1924, 224-25.

[19] Vilhelm Lundström, "Augustana-Synoden och svenskheten," *Allsvensk samling*, 16 April 1925, 4. Cf. Stephenson, *Religious Aspects*, 453-54.

[20] Vilhelm Lundström, "Den svenske veteranen," in his *Allsvenska linjer* (Göteborg, 1930), 97-100; Johannes Hoving, *Vasabarnens från Amerika trenne resor i fars och mors land 1924, 1929, 1933. Minnen och intryck* (Stockholm, 1935), esp. 23-24.

[21] *Augustana*, 14 May 1925, 310-11; 8 October 1925, 648; 3 September 1925, 570; 10 December 1925, 792-93; 24 July 1930, 488-89.

[22] *Lutheran Companion*, 2 February 1924, 75; Lindmark, *Swedish America*, 265, 273, 276-303, esp. 292; Hasselmo, *Amerikasvenska*, 63-72; my *Folk Divided*, 303.

[23] Nathan Söderblom, *Från Uppsala till Rock Island. En predikofärd i Nya världen* (Stockholm, 1924); Anna Söderblom, *An Amerikabok* (Stockholm. 1925), by the archbishop's wife; review of the latter in *Augustana*, 8 October 1925, 648; Karl Hildebrand and Axel Fredenholm, eds., *Svenskarna i Amerika*, 2 vols. (Stockholm, 1925-26); Fritz Henriksson, *Med Sveriges kronprinsar genom Amerika* (Stockholm, 1926). Cf. my *Folk Divided*, 283-301 passim, 277-81.

[24] Vilhelm Lundström, "Kring svenskar, svenskhet och svenskminnen i U.S.A.," *Till trettioårsdagen 1908 3/XII 1938* (Göteborg, 1938), 5-23. Cf. my *Folk Divided*, 284, 321.

THE TROUBLESOME LANGUAGE QUESTION

In a 1920 annual report, Pastor Andrew Anderson referred to the transition from Swedish to English in his church as "*den bekymmersamma språkfrågan.*"[1] The language change in immigrant churches, often accompanied by lengthy controversy, heated debate and profound emotions, was just that. Immigrants, who began to learn English immediately on their arrival, clung to Swedish in their worship services as long as possible. Struggle as they did, the new world language was to overtake them.

> Transplanted to American soil, the Swede was placed in an inexorable environment. He found himself in a society that mocked him and the institutions, customs, and language he had brought with him, a society so strong, moreover, that it must inevitably dominate him.[2]

My aim in this article is to examine and illustrate the general problem of establishing and sustaining a religious tradition in a "foreign tongue." I am interested in the relation between language, especially mother tongue, and faith. One small town church in Stambaugh, Michigan, Grace Covenant, and two large metropolitan churches in the Twin Cities, Salem Covenant and First Covenant, St. Paul, are included in the study. Little attention has been given to the problem of the language transition in immigrant churches.[3] Change is, of course, a constant process, but there are those *kairos* moments, here troublesome periods, in the history of the Americanization of the immigrant church. As Philip J. Anderson writes, "The transition from Swedish to English overshadowed all other difficulties in the Swedish-American denominations from 1900 to 1935."[4]

The church was for the immigrants the guardian of their native religious and cultural experience. They had to deal with the new language in the secular areas of life; in the holy space and time of worship they preferred their mother tongue. Marcus Lee Hansen notes that "The church was the first, the most important and the most significant institution that the immigrants established."[5] "The sphere of the church," agrees Alfred Fonkalsrud, "has been . . . the cultural cradle of Scandinavians in America."[6] Of course, some Swedish immigrants, lacking an interest in the Faith and the Church, found their lives centered on other social organizations.

The first-generation immigrants established their churches using their native language. Intermarriage, community outreach and the arrival of American-born families created the language problem. Being required to think, speak and understand in a new language was both difficult and distressful. Fortunately, as the years passed, some became bilingual and could translate sermons and hymns into English. For the immigrants themselves, however, the problem was not whether translations were available but the fact of translation itself. They wondered, do the new idioms and metaphors we are asked to use really mirror our inward faith and conversion experiences? Do prayers in English get through to God as well as those in Swedish?[7] Do the English lyrics really fit with the rhythmic cadences of the old hymn tunes?[8]

New and different words for the same human experiences carry disparate emotions. In his novel *The Settlers*, Wilhelm Moberg illustrates the point as he relates the last moments of young Swedish immigrant Arvid's life. Robert notices the little sign by the watering hole in the desert warning of death only after his friend, Arvid, has drunk the poisoned water.

> He had two names for death, each sounding very different to his ear: the Swedish word sounded hard and frightening and threatening: **Döden**! It would be the clarion call over earth on doomsday morning: Döööden! That word cut like an ax through bone and marrow. Its echo was fear, a sound without mercy, a wailing without comfort. But the English **death** sounded soft and peaceful, quiet and restful. It didn't call for an end to life in threatening and condemning sounds. Death was soft-voiced, merciful, it approached silently, kindly. It brought comfort and compassion to a person at the end of his life. Death—it was a whisper in the ear, it didn't frighten or terrify. It said in the kindest of words how things stood; it said in all friendliness: **Now you will die.**[9]

Hearing and using new words for old familiar events, objects, and actions was a common feature of immigrant experience. Contacts with the new culture—in daily business and work conversations, in church and school, through the newspapers, and so forth—hastened the acquisition of the new language.[10] Once families were established, the acculturation process was even more rapid and complicated. It soon became evident that the mother tongue of the immigrants was not, and could never be, the mother tongue of the their offspring. As Moberg writes in *The Last Letter Home*:

> . . . Father and sons already used different languages when they spoke with each other. The children more and more discarded their mother tongue for English—when he addressed them in Swedish they would reply in English. This seemed awkward to him and plainly askew. At first he tried to correct them, but by and by he became accustomed to it and after some time it no longer bothered him. There was nothing he could do about it, so perhaps it was better to say nothing. After all, his children were right; he must not hinder them from speaking their country's language.[11]

Congregations were often slow in coming to this insight. Pastors at first encouraged children to learn Swedish along with the religion of their parents, and set up "Swede schools." They usually were held during summer vacation and met in church basements, schoolhouses, or church sanctuaries. The usual subjects were Bible history, Luther's Catechism, and Swedish. The idea back of these schools was put succinctly in the slogan, "Language saves faith." In larger churches, a student would be hired to teach; in smaller ones, the pastor taught.[12] One Scandinavian pastor, the Rev. A. J. Tarpgaard, said, "If one were to have one's Christian life enriched, it would presently have to be accomplished in Danish. The important thing was to speak so that hearts were warmed."[13] George M. Stephenson appraised the Swede school within the Lutheran tradition in these words:

> In theory it was a school of religion, but in reality it was maintained to teach Swedish. . . . Many children as a result of this practice grew up with the idea that the Swedish language and salvation were one and inseparable. The devil himself could hardly have devised a better instrument than the Catechism for turning youth against the church and inspiring hatred for the Swedish language.[14]

59

Karl A. Olsson concludes that Swede schools had both values and serious drawbacks for Covenant churches:

> Much of this had ultimate value. It enriched the culture and linguistic perception of the children and gave them some understanding of the world-view of their parents. But as a measure for maintaining the character of the church it was futile and perhaps even harmful. It gave the children a parochially narrow view of the church of Christ, and it did not serve to universalize the Covenant ideal. If the first generation had devoted as much time and energy to learning English as they spent on teaching their children Swedish, the Covenant would have been ready earlier to carry its message to the American community.[15]

Whatever the short- and long-term values, English was increasingly replacing Swedish.[16] During World War I, many of the second generation found themselves in situations—military, political, social, academic, business, domestic, and work-related—that made the mastery of English, including the removal of any foreign accents, imperative. The second and third generations, born in America, were often embarrassed by the old folkways, the accents, and the broken English of their parents. Good jobs, they knew, were for those who could communicate fluently in the vernacular.

The transition from Swedish to English was particularly difficult in the morning service, the traditional Swedish "*högmässa*" (high mass), or the more standard, "*gudstjänst*" (Divine service). Holding Sunday school, confirmation classes, midweek prayer meetings, and the evening evangelistic services in English was one thing; conducting worship at 11 o'clock on Sunday morning in a "foreign tongue" was quite another.[17] For some immigrants, regardless of their fluency in English, giving up worship in Swedish was irreverent and inconceivable, like losing the Faith or being disloyal to Christ. Some, not entirely in humor, referred to Swedish as "The language of heaven." One little boy was certain that "Jesus was a Swede." The Swedish language, their mother tongue, was for them the locus of truth, reality, and knowledge.[18] Frans Ericsson's poem, "*Svenska språket*," makes the point:

> *På detta språk vi hälsades till världen;*
> *på det vi bådo fromt vår första bön.*

60

Det klingade i sång kring barndomshärden;
det tydde för oss världens kunskapsrön.[19]

Resistance to the new language was not just simple tenacity, but rather an earnest desire to retain and preserve the faith, values, and traditions of the homeland. It was not that they lacked confidence in, nor were embarrassed by, the old language, but rather because they had confidence in it, and wanted to preserve its sounds and rhythms, that the language issue became troublesome. In Lindmark's words, "The language was sacred and was not to be tampered with."[20]

Continued use of Swedish in worship made for confusion and disagreement among the first, second, and third generations.[21] A June 1926 resolution from the Covenant Church in Grand Rapids, Michigan, illustrates the situation: "Resolved that people who are unable to speak Swedish, but who are really children of God, and who wish to join, may be taken in as members."[22]

Confusion reigned also in the normal tasks of the preacher. The late Rev. Herbert Palmquist gives several illustrations, one of which is included here:

When one of our pastors [with limited English-language skills] was to have a funeral, he was asked to speak in English because there 'might be those present who do not understand the Swedish.' But when he looked over his congregation it appeared to him that it was composed entirely of familiar faces, and so he asked: 'Is there anyone here who does not understand Swedish?' One man raised his hand. 'I tell you afterwards,' said the preacher and went on in Swedish.[23]

A young seminarian, Albert Berg, is said to have conducted the very first English service at Spring Vale Baptist Church, a Minnesota immigrant congregation, in 1925. The response is recorded in its diamond jubilee book: "Needless to say, this aroused considerable controversy among the older members. As one of our older friends recalls, 'The Lord could not understand English at that time, you know.'"[24]

Virginia Bergman Peters, in a delightful essay, tells of her experience in the early days at the Covenant Church in Dawson, Minnesota. She writes:

When I was confirmed . . . all of the classes were in English but the services were still in Swedish. When the young people began to urge that services be changed to English, there was resistance. . . . When it was pointed out that since we were all American citizens living in America we should worship in our native tongue, [Grandfather Bergman] replied—not entirely in jest—'but I always assumed that God was Swedish.'[25]

Kermit Holmgren of Salem Covenant Church in Pennock, Minnesota, notes in an article, "I Remember," that:

When our church changed from Swedish to the English language it was one of the most difficult periods in our church history. Many of the older people spoke English only when they had to. . . I remember the heartache of the older people as they felt their worship of God was taken away. One of them said at a business meeting where it was voted to change another service to English, that it was like the little boy who cut off his dog's tail one inch at a time, so it wouldn't hurt so much.[26]

Some churches changed to English more smoothly and quickly than others. Location was the main factor responsible for the difference between those churches that experienced a gradual and stressful period of language change from those where the change occurred rapidly with little disruption. Generally, churches in rural and small town communities, less that 5,000 population, were slower to make the change, while metropolitan churches, once the issue was identified as a problem for mission, changed quickly.[27] Several factors are involved here—the ratio of immigrants to non-immigrants, cultural, socio-economic levels in the community and in the congregation.

Nils Hasselmo, writing about the values connected with the Swedish language and spirit, makes a salient point by stressing that language is more than an interchangeable linguistic communication code that can be switched on and off:

. . . Language represents history and traditions, home, parents, and childhood, religious and aesthetic ideals. It is a reminder of the homeland to the exile. It is a faithful friend in lonely moments, a travel companion and an escape. It is the tool whereby Swedish culture is spread and identified. It is the symbol of unity and joins the people scattered over the new continent.[28]

Beyond questions of the importance of the values held within the Swedish language for personal and national identity are those of denominational identity.[29] People feared that the immigrant church and/or denomination would lose its identity, integrity, and mission if and when the mother tongue was replaced by English. Once the faith was separated from language and nationality, the question became: What will happen to our original principles?

By entering a new and wider sphere of influence the Covenanters have also entered into a new competition and become exposed to new influences and perils which, if not guarded against, may divert the direction and character of the Mission Covenant from the principles and ideals on which it was founded, which constitute its very message and contribution to American religious life.[30]

New prospects and new perils attended the abandonment of the Swedish language. Once faith was detached from the old language it was free to move in new directions, one of which was to take on the language and doctrines of Fundamentalism. Religious fights with science, evolution especially, raged in the 20s and 30s, and for some the language and doctrinal spirit of that fight replaced the older connection of language and faith.[31]

To summarize, immigrants faced a difficult period of language transition in their churches. They accepted English more readily in services other than Sunday morning worship. Large metropolitan churches changed more quickly than rural or small town churches. Swedes in non-urban areas, because of the ratio to non-Swedes, formed more visible, closely-knit associations and retained the Swedish language in their churches long after it was necessary for general communication. They often lagged behind denominational decisions. In the Covenant, for example, by a vote of 131-47 English was adopted as the official language of the Church in 1928.[32] Not many local congregations, urban or non-urban, were all-English by then. Virginia Bergman Peters puts the ambiguity of the situation well:

The change should, perhaps, have come years earlier. Surely it

63

would be an anachronism to continue the use of a 'foreign' language in American services but sometimes I wonder if those of us who were privileged to worship in two languages had recourse to a deeper, wider understanding of the Word than those who never had to puzzle over whether God was Swedish or English.[33]

In the course of my research I have had contacts with many who lived through the language transition in immigrant churches.[34] Though I deal mainly with Covenant churches, the language question posed a common problem for every immigrant church whether it was Swedish Baptist, German Catholic,[35] Danish Lutheran,[36] Greek Orthodox, and so on. "Sooner or later in every denomination the language question arose, and the proceedings of church conventions and the columns of the official organs were filled with debates and resolutions."[37] The emotions involved in adjusting to the new language were much the same whatever the denomination.

Stambaugh, Michigan: A Case Study

The Swedish Evangelical Mission Covenant (now Grace Covenant) Church, my home church, in the Upper Peninsula of Michigan struggled for many years with the language issue. This church may be taken as an illustration of the troublesome nature of the language issue in rural or small town immigrant churches in the 30s and 40s.

Stambaugh Covenant was, and is, located in a relatively small population center. Four small towns—Iron River, Stambaugh, Caspian, and Gaastra, along with the surrounding rural areas make up the community; and it had a combined population of less than 10,000 in 1930. The main occupations were farming, mining and logging. Italian, Finnish, Swedish, French, English, and other nationalities settled the area. In addition to the Covenant Church, several Lutheran immigrant congregations were established.

The composition of the Covenant congregation in Stambaugh was obviously a factor in the prolonged use of Swedish on Sunday mornings. James E. Erickson, a son of the church, has established a Hjulsjö parish (Örebro *län*)—Stambaugh, Michigan, kinship connection.[38] Of the fifty-nine individuals he identifies in this group, some were members of, or attended, the Covenant Church, while others became involved in local Lutheran, Baptist, Presbyterian, and Seventh

Day Adventist congregations. Although members of the Covenant Church came from other parts of Sweden as well, the Hjulsjö contingent was a significant, active presence in the church. A Norwegian, Thomas Thompson (born Tollak Tønnessen in Egersund, Norway), married to Hilda Maria Andersdotter from Hjulsjö, became a member in 1930 and manifested an abiding appreciation for Swedish Sunday morning worship. He died on 2 January 1944.

Mission Covenant Church, Stambaugh, Michigan. (Courtesy of Elder M. Lindahl.)

That the original immigrants settled and remained in close association within this small community, was a key factor in their clinging to Swedish into the 40s. The economy of the area was stable, the mines and lumber camps were operating, and there was little movement to the cities. Cultural events and offerings in the area were limited, and drinking was a problem.[39] At its founding in 1883, the Swedish Mission Church in Stambaugh conducted all services in Swedish. No agitation for a change to English seems to have occurred during the first two decades of the twentieth century. The concern was the spiritual welfare of Swedish immigrants and their children. Swede schools were held to insure that the second generation would know the Swedish language, church history, and Luther's catechism. The real push for English, along with the resistance to it, came later.

The following dates mark certain shifts and changes in the language transition process in Stambaugh:

3 September 1925: One morning service will be held each month in English.[40]

2 May 1932: All Sunday evening services, Bible classes, and Sunday school will be held in English; Sunday mornings will continue in Swedish.

15 December 1933: It is decided to have every third Sunday morning in English. Also, communion will now be in English.

2 July 1934: A committee is appointed to translate the church constitution and by-laws into English. The translation is accepted on 28 January 1935.

1934-1939: The language issue comes up now and again during this period. Suggestions to hold all Sunday morning services in English are made and countered. No formal decisions are made.

1 January 1940: A motion to have every first Sunday morning of the month in English is passed.

1 January 1941: A motion to have every other Sunday morning in English is defeated by a vote of 22-16 (membership, 96).

1 January 1942: A motion to hold more English Sunday morning services is defeated; the status quo of every first and third Sunday in English, is retained.

1 January 1943: A motion to have all Sunday morning services in English is defeated by a vote of 11-7 (membership, 89).

21 August 1944: At a special congregational meeting, a motion to hold all Sunday morning services in English is passed. Special Swedish worship services will be held at 3:00 on Sunday afternoons.[41]

The New Year's Day annual congregational meetings in the late 30s and early 40s usually moved along quite cordially until we came to the language issue. I recall that each year sides would form, lively debate occur, and the members who stayed to the end would leave hopelessly divided and embittered. The strong emotions would quiet down in time, only to resurface whenever the language issue came up during the year.

At these annual meetings the pro-Swedish group argued that by giving up the mother tongue, personal Christian experience would suffer, the church would lose its roots, heritage, and distinctiveness and simply become like all the rest of the American churches.[42] Some of the young people agreed with this position. They argued that the older immigrants had founded this church and that their descendants must respect and honor them by keeping Sunday morning worship in Swedish. The pro-English group, on the other hand, argued that retaining Swedish would prevent us from being a credible evangelical witness, would stagnate the church, and would mean the loss of many young people who were attending our Sunday school and youth programs. They pointed out that almost everyone, except for one or two, could communicate in English, and after all we do live in America.[43] Thus, the congregation faced a dilemma: Use all English and lose the spiritual quality of the worship; use Swedish and lose the young people. The arguments changed little from year to year.

Clergymen were caught in the middle. Pastor Carl Olson, who served from the spring of 1923 to August 1932, preached in Swedish only. Pastor Robert Sturdy, who came to Stambaugh in the fall of 1932 and served until December 1939, was bilingual and attracted local people both by his Swedish and English homiletic skills. The same held for Pastor Daniel Bloomdahl, who served Stambaugh from December 1939 to November 1947. More the scholar and less the evangelist than Sturdy, Bloomdahl also spoke both languages fluently. Both Sturdy and Bloomdahl, as far as I remember, promoted and supported the moves to full use of English.

Signs increasingly pointed to the fact that the future of the church lay with the new language. As time went on, Swedish Sunday morning services were not as well attended as the English Sunday evening services. The choir that sang on Sunday morning was composed almost entirely of adults, whereas the one on Sunday evening was larger, more lively, and composed of many young people. Singing in the morning was more stately, to the accompaniment of a pump organ, while in the evening service, it was informal, with a variety of instruments and groups—string band, men's chorus, duets, trios, and quartets. The vitality of the church shifted to Sunday evenings. Young people, restricted by pietistic rules against movies, cards, and dances, eagerly attended the evening services to be with their friends. Church became their social as well as their religious life.

There was a division of opinion in the congregation on whether second-generation members ought to require their non-Swedish speaking children to attend Swedish morning worship. Approximately 15% of the non-Swedish-speaking young people were required to attend, and I was in that group. What occupied us during these "foreign" services? Of those surveyed, many indicated positively that they sang with the congregation and found the Swedish hymns edifying and enjoyable. Negatively, many spent the time daydreaming about sports, dinner, dates for the evening, school work, and an afternoon at the lake. Many of us thought about the lucky ones who were excused from the service. One slept; another found the whole affair confusing; a third watched the clock. While some counted ceiling squares, others searched the little hymnbook, *Sions Basun*, for interesting sounding Swedish words such as, *"icke," "sex," "barn," "korset,"* etc.

What did the other 85% do on Sunday mornings when the services were in Swedish? Some bought the Sunday paper and went home to read the comics. Others met their friends downtown at Dr. Vilas's drugstore or Kemp's grocery to talk, joke around, drink cokes and laugh together, coming back to church just as the Swedish service concluded. One went home to put the finishing touches on dinner, while another made preparations for afternoon baseball, swimming, and a drive. Others in this group, after attending the Covenant Sunday school, found their way to different Protestant churches in Stambaugh or Iron River. Some members were attracted by other pastors—Charles Erickson of First Lutheran, Stewart Warner of First Presbyterian, Charles Cookingham of the Methodist Church, and Minnie Nelson of First Baptist. This resulted in young people attending Sunday school and confirmation at the Covenant Church but then simply dropping out and/or joining other groups.[44]

Two aspects of the Swedish worship experience might be mentioned. Prayers were most often spontaneous; the pastor would simply call on someone. When an oldtimer, like Thomas (Tom) Thompson mentioned above, stood to pray his impassioned cadences reflected deep personal experiences and a close walk with God. He and others seemed to approach the Holy of Holies, *nådens tron* (the throne of grace), very naturally and intimately. Using English would have been most unnatural and difficult for these immigrants, a consummate impoverishment of the Spirit. "That people who were able to express themselves so eloquently in their native tongue should be subjected to the task of speaking in another tongue seems, indeed, cruel. It was like clipping the bird's wings."[45]

Another memorable part of the Swedish worship services was the music. A string band, choirs, solos, duets, trios, quartets, and the accordion-like sounds from an old pump organ kept the folk air. The hymnals contained only the lyrics. The lilt of the Swedish words and tunes, tempos, and harmonies were deeply felt. When those pioneers, after a hard week of honest toil in the mines, on the farms, or at their trades, opened their worship with the song *"Sabbatsdag,"* one knew they believed they had crossed the threshold from the secular into the Sacred.

Sabbatsdag, hur skön du är,
Skänkt av Gud, jag har dig kär;
Kom, o kom än en gång
Samla oss till bön och sång!

Efter arbetveckans strid
Få vi sitta ned i frid
Vid vår Faders rika bord,
Lyssnande till nådens ord.[46]

A. L. Skoog's fine English translation hardly does justice to the religious feelings, the aesthetic values, and the spiritual experience of these immigrants. The holy day, for example, in Swedish is addressed lovingly and familiarly as *"du,"* i.e., "Thou," not as a neutral "it:" "Sunday, how beautiful You are, given by God, I hold you dear."

Swedish-American traditions continued into the 40s. *Julotta*, the traditional early Christmas morning service, was held in Stambaugh each year. Also, a *"gubbfest,"* (old men's party) was scheduled annually at 8:30 on New Year's Eve. First- and second-generation men baked cakes, made cookies, and served coffee in the lower auditorium. As part of the watchnight service that followed, men and boys put on the program, singing Swedish hymns and playing the organ, violin, and guitar. An annual fixture on this occasion was Art Thompson, Tom's son, playing the mandolin.

The language transition at Stambaugh, protracted as it was, did not stunt the growth of the church in the long run. It never experienced a split, and today (1995) Grace Covenant thrives as a strong, vital congregation of 225 members with Swedish and non-Swedish names. Several chapels were established in outlying areas—Bates, Maple Grove, Pioneer, Gibbs City, and Tipler. In time these chapels were closed or sold and their people, along with those from the immigrant Mission Church in Beechwood, were invited to join Grace Covenant. Although some non-Swedes were lost to the group during the troublesome period, others then and now, seem to feel at home and appreciate the traditions and folkways of the original immigrant culture. Confirmation and infant baptism, along with child dedication, are still celebrated. Evidences of the Swedish roots—now mostly in the serving of certain Swedish foods, *julotta* (now on Christmas Eve), and some folk celebrations continue to identify the church locally. The experience of Stambaugh appears to be typical of many other rural and small town Covenant churches.

69

Two Metropolitan Churches in the Twin Cities

Salem Covenant, now in New Brighton, Minnesota, began in 1886 as a witness to a large Scandinavian community. Founded in 1888, as the Swedish Evangelical Mission Covenant Church of Northeast Minneapolis, it was located in an urban area around Jefferson and 17th, just across from a casket factory. With the construction of a larger new building on Central Ave N.E., the church served a greater community—Swedes and non-Swedes—during the years 1900 to 1970. The church seated about 800. A chapel in Columbia Heights was founded during this time.

The congregation began almost immediately to establish, fund, and maintain a Swede school to preserve the Swedish language. Pastor C. V. Bowman, in a letter dated 2 January 1905, stated:

> In our activities, it is coming more and more to the point where we need to make special efforts to interest the young people growing up. Children among us, although born of Swedish parents are not familiar enough with the mother tongue. It is a problem difficult to solve—how we shall handle that, what we must do, or what it would take to reach their hearts and win their interest. While we wait for a fortunate solution to that question we should show these young people friendship and confidence as long as possible.[47]

Swede schools were held at Salem during the wait for a "fortunate solution." They served a twin function—as a way to insure an evangelical outreach for new immigrants and a way to prevent assimilation into the secular culture. Teachers were recruited largely from North Park Seminary, and the pattern of offerings was similar to what has been mentioned above. By 1920, however, the Swedish school solution had been discontinued.

The transition to greater use of English in the services, begun in the late 20s, followed the common pattern of starting with English in the Sunday school, confirmation, business meetings, and so on. The leadership provided by the Rev. Clarence Nelson took some of the pain from the struggle. As of 1 October 1938 all services, including Sunday morning worship, were to be held in English. Swedish services were conducted in the lower auditorium for several years thereafter, with an occasional special Swedish morning service in the sanctuary. The entire transition process took about a decade.

First Covenant Church of Saint Paul, Minnesota, illustrates another transition pattern. Founded in 1874, the church built a "First Mission House," then a "Second Mission House" at what is now Payne Avenue and Kenny Road in St. Paul. In 1902, the congregation moved into "the Tabernacle" at Edgerton and Minnehaha. It was in this location, serving a population of some 25,000 people, that the move to all English occurred.

The language transition was relatively brief, less than a decade, and fairly uncomplicated. One might label the transition process here as "bilingual," as the resistance against, and the push for, English were met by the building of several chapels nearby. For example, in 1921, the Phalen Park Chapel at Earl and Hawthorne, with all services in English, was built. While the ministry there was mostly to those living in that area, some from the Tabernacle attended. The pastor, A. E. Palmquist writes in the "bilingual" 50th anniversary book,[48]

> Although many of the members were still Swedish immigrants, a large part of the church membership consisted of young people who knew very little of the Swedish language. Because some of these young people were leaving for English speaking churches, it became evident that some English services needed to be held in The Tabernacle where most of the members attended services. At first there was one meeting a month in English on a Sunday evening, then two Sunday evenings in English, and later there were morning services in English every other Sunday. But it was not until Pastor Bolin arrived in 1934 that all of the regular services were conducted in English.

In 1930 business meetings were conducted in both languages. However, with the election of a new secretary, Oscar Goethe, who took the job on the condition that he could use English, no minutes were written in Swedish after 16 February 1931.

Though Pastor Bolin, as noted in the above quotation, arrived in 1934, the complete change to English took time.[49] On 1 January 1936 by a vote of 170-38, a decision was made to hold every other morning service in English. The Easter Sunday morning service on 7 March 1938 was in English. From that time on, with the exception of an occasional bilingual *julotta* and special afternoon meetings, all services in the Tabernacle were in English. The membership at First Covenant in 1938 was 775.

And what about "Swede schools" at First Covenant? As far as we can determine, this temporary transition technique was never used here. Pastor Palmquist wrote in 1924, at a time when Swede schools were common in other immigrant churches, "The language question is far from being the most important one; it has never been for us a burning question but we seek to adjust to it in accordance with necessity."[50] Apparently Swede schools were not considered necessary in this bilingual, pragmatic approach.

*

I have attempted to show the importance of language in the experience of immigrant church people. More than a vehicle for communication, the Swedish language expressed for them their deepest spiritual truths, their sense of reality, and their religious knowledge claims. It had emotive as well as cognitive significance. The question for many was whether the spirituality of old world piety could and would survive in pluralistic, secular America. For others, the question of mission to the unchurched was more prominent.

The transitions at Salem Covenant, New Brighton, and First Covenant, St. Paul, differ from one another and, as one can see, also from the experience of Grace Covenant in Stambaugh and other non-urban immigrant congregations. The larger population context demanded faster, more direct action. Resistance to giving up the mother tongue obviously existed, but it was met with different strategies. Adjustment to the declining number of immigrants was made in larger churches in a relatively short period. In the large metropolitan churches, immigrants were able to translate their cherished tradition into foreign idioms more rapidly than their non-urban cousins.

But not all immigrant churches survived. Some were simply not willing or able to integrate the old religious experience with the new wine of the land. As someone put it, referring to the situation in North Dakota:

Churches were established because Swedish was popular;
Churches were closed because Swedish was unpopular.

Although too simple sociologically, these balanced lines make a relevant point about the role of language in the beginnings—and in the endings—of immigrant churches.

For the generation born in Sweden, the mother tongue meant security in an alien setting and an effective Gospel witness to arriving immigrants; for the descendants, the old language and tradition became a confusing and troublesome problem. Partial solutions, compromises, and creative blends worked for a time. In the end, nothing short of abandoning the old rhythmic cadences was feasible. The new, enriched and invigorated by the old, was a better way—the only way—for an immigrant church to survive in the new land.

NOTES

[1] "The troublesome language question." Quoted from *This is the Lord's Doings*, 1880 Diamond Jubilee Anniversary, Mission Covenant Church (Grand Rapids, Michigan, Jubilee Publication Committee, 1955), n. pag.

[2] George M. Stephenson, *The Religious Aspects of Swedish Immigration* (Minneapolis: University of Minnesota, 1932), v.

[3] Stephenson's classic work, *The Religious Aspects of Swedish Immigration* is the most comprehensive study of the Swedish immigrant churches—Lutheran, Covenant, Methodist, Mormons, and others. Nils Hasselmo deals with the problem of transition in a general way in "Language in Exile," *The Swedish Immigrant Community in Transition: Essays in honor of Dr. Conrad Bergendoff*, eds. J. Inverne Dowie and Ernest M. Espelie (Rock Island: Augustana Historical Society, 1963), pp. 121-46. Sture Lindmark's *Swedish America, 1914-1932* (Stockholm: Läromedelsförlaget, 1971) is a study of the group consciousness of Swedish America. The demographical statistics he gives in Chapters IX and XI are especially helpful. The quartet of historical fictional works by Wilhelm Moberg, *The Emigrants, Unto A Good Land, The Settlers,* and *The Last Letter Home*, Trans. by Gustaf Lannestock (New York: Popular Library, 1978) give an accurate and insightful portrait of emigrant life and transitional problems.

[4] Philip J. Anderson, *A Precious Heritage: A Century of Mission in the Northwest 1884-1984* (Minneapolis: The Northwest Conference, 1984), p. 84.

[5] Marcus Lee Hansen, *The Problem of the Third Generation Immigrant* (Rock Island, Ill.: Augustana Historical Society, 1938), p. 15.

[6] Alfred O. Fonkalsrud in collaboration with Beatrice Stevenson, *The Scandinavian-American* (Minneapolis: K.C. Holter Publishing Co., 1915), p. 138.

[7] Two illustrations of this point: an older friend of mine is reported to have prayed earnestly in Swedish on his deathbed. His son said that this was the first time he had ever heard his father, a second-generation Swedish American, speak in Swedish. Also, Robert C. Ostergren, in *A Community Transplanted: The Trans-Atlantic Experience of a Swedish Immigrant Settlement in the Upper Middle West, 1835-1915* (Madison: University of Wisconsin Press, 1988), p. 277, tells of ". . . The wife of one member of the church council is supposed to have exclaimed on hearing the issue [using English in worship]: 'Can you pray in English?'"

[8] For example, "All Hail to Thee, O Blessed Morn," simply does not capture the mystique of *"Var hälsad, sköna morgonstund."*

[9] Moberg, *The Settlers*, p. 280.

[10] See *Perspectives on Swedish Immigration*, Ed. by Nils Hasselmo (Duluth: University of

Minnesota Press, 1978) for a presentation of the dynamics of the "speech economy" model. Often Swedes clustered together into what Hasselmo calls "Swedish language islands." English was the language of the mainstream surrounding these islands. "Whenever the Swedish-Americans stepped outside the confines of their own families, neighborhoods, and institutions, they were confronted with English as the informal and formal spoken language and as the written language of the land." p. 232.

[11] Moberg, *The Last Letter Home*, p. 239.

[12] Dorothy Burton Skårdal, in *The Divided Heart* (Lincoln: University of Nebraska Press, 1974) notes that children of the immigrants did not have the same feelings attached to Swedish words as did the immigrants. "Those who grew up in exclusively Scandinavian settlements were usually bilingual, but even those who spoke their parents' language could not share the feelings of their parents toward the European tongue, subject as the children were to powerful pressures towards use of English from the surrounding environment." p. 90. Hasselmo in *Perspectives on Swedish Immigration*, p. 233, makes a similar point. "In spite of some concerted efforts to provide Swedish language instruction and instruction in Swedish history and Swedish traditions in the 'Swede schools,' many Swedish-American children probably had a rather limited literacy in their 'mother tongue' and a very limited familiarity with the cultural traditions of their 'fatherland.'"

[13] Quoted in Enok Mortensen, *The Danish Lutheran Church in America* (Philadelphia: Lutheran Church of America, 1967), p. 174

[14] Stephenson, *Religious Aspects*, p. 410.

[15] Karl A. Olsson, *By One Spirit* (Chicago: Covenant Press, 1962), p. 486.

[16] World War I brought significant changes to the Covenant Church in Warren, Minnesota. "Up until the war, Swedish had been the official language in all services of the church, even the Sunday school classes were conducted in what was called 'the language of Heaven.' However, in the middle twenties the influx of Swedish immigrants almost came to an end with the restricted immigration quotas. Outreach had to be made to English-speaking friends and neighbors. It was not easy to make this transition, but by the end of the 30s and early 40s almost all services were conducted in the English language." Swedish prayer meetings were held every other Thursday evening as late as 1945, and a Swedish language adult class continued into the 50s. *100th Anniversary Evangelical Covenant Church, Warren, Minnesota* (1982), p. 14.

[17] According to George Stevenson in *Religious Aspects*, p. 291, the Covenant held out for Swedish as *"gudstjänstspråk"* longer than the other Swedish immigrant denominations.

[18] Hasselmo, in *Perspectives on Swedish Immigration*, p. 235, says, "The Swedish language became a symbol for the Swedish-Americans. It represented the customs and tradition of their daily lives, their religion, their history—their very identity as thinking and feelings humans beings. In the words of J. S. Carlson...'The *spirit* of a people lives and dwells . . . in its language. . .'"

[19] "In this language we were welcomed into this world; in it we piously said our first prayer. It rang out in song at our childhood's hearth; it interpreted the knowledge of the world for us." Hasselmo, "Language in Exile," p. 127.

[20] Lindmark, *Swedish America*, p. 266.

[21] Much of the defence of Swedish was made in a blended language, in what is now called variously *"mixat språk,"* "Folkloristic" American-Swedish, or "Swengelish."

[22] *This is the Lord's Doings*, Mission Covenant Church, Grand Rapids, Michigan.

[23] Herbert Palmquist, *The Wit and Wisdom of Our Fathers* (Chicago: Covenant Press, 1967), p. 113.

[24] *Spring Vale Baptist Church, 1886-1961*, n. pag.

[25] *Dawson Covenant Church, 1889-1989*, n. pag.

[26] *Crowning A Century, 1871-1971*, Salem Covenant Church, Pennock, Minnesota, Centennial Publication Committee, 1971, p. 52.

[27] I estimate the average period for the change as 10 years in metropolitan churches and some 16-35 years in the rural and small town churches. And there are exceptions, such as a large metropolitan congregation, the Minneapolis Laestadian Lutheran Church in Plymouth, Minn., which as of 1995 continues to have sermons in Finnish on the first and third Sundays of the month.

[28] Hasselmo, *Perspectives on Swedish Immigration*, p. 235.

[29] Charles Milton Strom in "The Swedish Evangelical Mission Covenant Church of America: A Study of Immigrant Acculturation" (M.A. thesis, University of California, Davis, 1990) argues that the reluctance to adopt English was not a matter of simple nationalism, but was due to the belief immigrants had that American churches were dominated by modernist theology and hedonism. Their continued use of Swedish helped them to preserve evangelical faith and keep the negative American influences at a distance.

[30] *Covenant Memories, Golden Jubilee, Swedish Evangelical Mission Covenant, 1885-1935* (Chicago: Covenant Book Concern, 1935), p. 101.

[31] See Karl A. Olsson's works *By One Spirit* and *A Family of Faith* (1975) for discussions of the impact of these controversies on Covenant identity.

[32] Stephenson, *Religious Aspects*, p. 292.

[33] Virginia Bergman Peters, *Dawson Covenant Church*, n. pag.

[34] Minneapolis/St. Paul, Pennock, Warren, Viking, Trimont, Mankato, and Dawson, Minnesota; Silver Hill, Alabama; Grand Rapids, Northport, Stambaugh, Michigan; etc. Particularly useful were various church jubilee books celebrating golden, diamond, or centennial anniversaries.

[35] "For a Catholic, to leave his neighborhood and church with no assurance of finding another German-speaking parish was tantamount to abandoning his religion." Jay Dolan, *The Immigrant Church* (London: University of Notre Dame Press, 1983), p. 41.

[36] One Danish Lutheran pastor, Benedik Nordentoft, one-time president of Grand View College, wrote that leaving the mother tongue was a sin against the 4th commandment. "You sin against God and man by abandoning the mother tongue. How can you have the heart to do it? How can you sadden your elders so? How in the future will you be able to face your children without blushing when they ask you why you severed the continuity of your ancestry and permitted them to grow up in ignorance and without having heard the sacred sound of the mother tongue through which generations before you have expressed their sorrows and joys?" Quoted from Mortensen, *The Danish Lutheran Church in America*, p. 187.

[37] Marcus Lee Hansen, *The Immigrant in America History* (Cambridge: Harvard University Press, 1948), p. 203.

[38] James E. Erickson, "The Hjulsjö (Öre.) to Stambaugh, MI Migration Axis," *Swedish American Genealogist*, 11 (1991): 1-33.

[39] Amusements were limited. H. Arnold Barton in *Letters from the Promised Land* (Minneapolis: University of Minnesota Press, 1975, p. 271) prints letters from an Iron River settler, George F. Erickson, who came to the area in 1909. Erickson lived there for some forty years and in 1911 wrote to a friend in Sweden who had asked about what people did on the long winter evenings. "There is a so-called Electric Theater here where they have shows on Saturday and Sunday evenings, but that is all. . . . In

this little town [Iron River] with maybe forty-five hundred inhabitants there are twelve saloons, and all of them do good business. Five minutes from here is another town [Stambaugh] . . . with two thousand inhabitants, and there they have thirty saloons. From this you can understand that there must be a lot of drinking when there are so many saloons and that there are good profits in it. . ."

[40] The motion was: *"Vidare beslöts att vi hålla ett engelskt möte en gång i månaden."*

[41] Pastor Bloomdahl's remarks at that special congregational meeting are summarized in the minutes: "He pointed out that three families (about 15 people) among our members were automatically excluded [from Sunday morning services] and were worshipping with other churches as a result. He also suggested that this was not a move to oust the Swedish entirely, but merely to reserve the regular Sunday services for English and avoid confusion among worshippers. Our pastor also suggested that we conduct a Swedish service in our church, once a month, and one Swedish cottage meeting per month. . . ."

[42] Virginia Dawson Peters, *Dawson Covenant Church*, n. pag., "I recall people saying something like: 'Soon there will be no one left who understands 'Tryggare kan ingen vara än Guds lilla barnaskara.' It will be sung in English but it won't be the same. I mourn the passing of something cherished and deeply meaningful.'"

[43] Lindmark, *Swedish America*, pp. 192-93, "The census of 1930 indicates that Swedish Americans learned English easily. In 1930 only 1.5 percent of all Swedish-born over 10 years of age could not speak English. . . ." In the same census, ". . . only 1.5 percent of all Swedish-born over 10 years of age were illiterate. . . . Compared with other immigrants the number of illiterate Swedes was percentage-wise among the lowest."

[44] How many is hard to say. I have no statistics on the numbers of young people and non-Swedish-speaking adults who were lost to the Covenant Church in Stambaugh during this time. Writing about the Covenant at large, Karl A. Olsson states that ". . . hundreds of thousands of American children who poured through Covenant Sunday schools were never won for Christ or integrated into his body. For them the Sunday school was a way station; it never became a home" *(By One Spirit*, p. 492).

[45] *This is the Lord's Doings*, n. pag.

[46] "Sabbath day of rest and cheer! / Day divine, to me so dear! / Come, o come to old and young, / Gath'ring all for prayer and song. Now the week of toil is o'er, / And in peace we sit once more / In Thy presence, gracious Lord, / List'ning to Thy holy Word." This singing tradition has been kept alive through the labors of one of the sons of the Stambaugh Church, the late Rev. J. Irving Erickson, who served on the Covenant Hymnal Commission and was a key person nationally in the preservation of songs from the Swedish heritage. See especially the articles Erickson wrote for *Pietisten* until his death on 12 December 1992.

[47] Quoted from church records.

[48] The book, titled *Minneskrift, 1874-1924. Historik över Svenska Evangeliska Lutherska Missionsförsamlingen, St. Paul, Minnesota*, has 43 pages in Swedish and 25 in English.

[49] The 100th anniversary book, *First Covenant Church, 1874-1974*, Ethel Arvidson, ed., n. pag., does make the point that, ". . . for the next few years [following 1931] the question of adopting the English language for all services became a 'burning question' in the congregation."

[50] *Ibid.*

WEIGHING THE STARS
AND HEARING THE WORD:
CONRAD BERGENDOFF'S IDEA OF CHRISTIAN
HIGHER EDUCATION AT AUGUSTANA COLLEGE
AND THEOLOGICAL SEMINARY

ANN BOADEN

I believe that we can have eyes and ears open to every fact which the physical and social sciences can bring us, and it is my hope that in some measure our own faculty will lead to an enlargement of the knowledge of the world. But as we break up the atom or weigh the stars or discover the secrets of organisms, let us also be trained to spiritual discernment of Him Who put the atoms together and upholds the stars and awakens the life of each day and night. . . .[1]

With these words, delivered to a packed chapel on a fall morning (1 October 1936) Conrad Bergendoff launched his presidency of Augustana College and Theological Seminary. Throughout nearly three decades of heading the joint institutions and then the college alone, three decades tumultuous with social and economic change, Bergendoff never lost this vision of Christian education—and never flagged in the energy with which he pursued it.

*

I first bumped into Conrad Bergendoff in a swimming pool. Literally. It was the summer of 1975. Doing my usual frenetic blind crawl down lane 2 of Augustana's Olympic-length facility, I splashed up against a firm resistance that was not the wall. It was Dr. Bergendoff.

I was not so blind that I did not know what I had done. Anyone who has attended Augustana College from 1935 to 1995 knows the face and the name. Spluttering to an upright position, I felt a hand steady me. I looked up to see a still-firm (at the age of 79) torso, a mane of white hair, twinkling blue eyes, a smile both amused and kind. For the next half hour we stood in the pool and talked about my doctoral dissertation, which I sometimes felt I was crawling through blindly, too. When I climbed out of the pool with crumpled fingers, I felt steadied in my thesis as well.

I include this personal recollection for two reasons: first, because it is, I believe, paradigmatic of the man I have come to know and love since that day—a man who balances health of body, mind, and spirit, one who can discuss literature in the steamy echoes of a swimming pool. Many people flailing blindly at various endeavors have bumped into him, and to them he has been without fail courteous, firm, often amused, and discerningly kind. Many he has steadied. Many, perhaps most, have come to admire and love him, and most, like me, welcome the chance to testify to that experience.

And I use the anecdote to define the scope and method of this article. It is not an exhaustive record of Dr. Bergendoff's professional life as President of Augustana College and Theological Seminary, but rather a portrait of that life, grounded in personal experience with the man himself. The way I have known him is through his connection with Augustana College, and so that is the world this article will emphasize. But, as I hope to show, Dr. Bergendoff's vision is holistic; his idea of Christian education embraced both college and seminary, and their ultimate division was something he neither anticipated nor approved.

*

Conrad Bergendoff was just two months shy of his forty-first birthday when he succeeded Dr. Gustav Andreen in 1936. Already he had compiled an impressive record of service to the Church. Born in Nebraska and raised in Connecticut, he had graduated from Augustana College in 1915, at the age of 19, and returned a year later, after earning his M.A. at the University of Pennsylvania, to teach English, education, and to coach debate. During 1917-1918 he attended the Lutheran Theological Seminary, Philadelphia, and in 1921 he received his B.D. degree from Augustana Seminary. He studied at major universities both here and abroad: Chicago, Columbia, Uppsala, Lund, Oxford, and Berlin, and received his doctorate from Chicago in 1928. His activities in the Church ranged from traveling as friend and assistant to Swedish Archbishop Nathan Söderblom to serving as pastor of Salem Lutheran Church, the oldest Augustana Synod

78

congregation on Chicago's south side. These experiences influenced his thinking about both education and institutional administration.

Bergendoff's association with Archbishop Söderblom, as well as his doctoral study of Olavus Petri, had convinced him that Lutheran theology mandated certain attitudes about life and especially education. The sacred and the secular interpenetrate; one cannot be "broken off" from the other without distortion. Examining other Christian colleges of the 1930s, he saw two models, both of which he rejected: one, in the name of scientific objectivity, severing ties with the originating church bodies; the other, closing off areas of knowledge to keep doctrine unsullied. The first he found not simply impossible but logically inconsistent: no institution, he argued, can purvey ideologically sanitized knowledge, because teaching method and approach embody ideology—they transmit conviction. The question is what sort of conviction an institution will transmit. The first model implies that scientific method is the only legitimate approach to truth; the second, that science threatens religion. In Bergendoff's view, both stances falsify the nature of knowledge and the ends of education. If God's word in Christ be the center of created reality, no approach to that reality can dislodge it, and no purely inductive procedure can discern it. Poetry, art, music, philosophy, sacred scriptures—the reach of the liberated imagination—are not simply attractive adjuncts to scientific inquiry but necessary complements to its methods. "An education which consists of fragments broken off the circumference of the circle of knowledge is something less than an education whose every segment and part refer to a center which holds the circle together," he concludes.[2] In the same vein he insists that theology must translate from cloistered proposition to concrete engagement with the world.

The university as he came to know it both in Europe and the United States provided an institutional pattern for the kind of education Bergendoff envisioned. An urbane and sophisticated scholar, he had found the university environment congenial. A churchman who frequently consulted New Testament texts in their original language—on one leg of his travels with Söderblom, the archbishop asked him, "Do you happen to have a Greek testament?" and Bergendoff produced the one he always carried—he could neither understand nor condone those "streams of Protestant thought" that contain "a concealed antagonism to all higher learning, a sort of hidden suspicion that education and piety do not mix very well."[3] For Bergendoff, Christian higher education demanded readiness and rigor in all intellectual pursuits. Recently (1995) he commented that the earliest founders of Augustana envisioned a university, an educational system comprising colleges of various academic disciplines, and including graduate study. In this model, college and seminary fit together. Recalling the 1948 split between the two—a trauma and turning point in his career—he added ruefully, "Oh well, you can always dream impossible things." But both the idea and the term, season his discourse in the first part of his presidency. ". . . Is that not a true university where all that man can know of heaven and earth is unified into a whole?" he asks in his inaugural address. A decade later he chastises the Lutheran seminaries for "drawing away from the university model."[4]

If his idea of the university was shaped by his intellectual and spiritual experiences, his pastoral work may have suggested the model of the school as parish. As president he established a relationship with faculty, staff, and students not unlike that of a minister with his parishioners. He continued the traditional metaphor used to describe the college community—the "Augustana family"—and terminology that identified teaching as a Christian vocation—faculty were "called" rather than "hired" to teach. Repeatedly he insisted that teaching at Augustana is a form of Christian service. He delivered sermons regularly, to the assembled "congregation" of the entire school—students, faculty, administration, and staff—in daily chapel services. These "chapel talks" still provide centering memories for graduates who heard them. He cared for his "family." No faculty member presented a paper, published an article, or even conducted an unusually successful class without a congratulatory note from Dr. Bergendoff; no member of the "family" contracted an illness, lost a loved one, or experienced discouragement without a word from Dr. Bergendoff. He and Mrs. Bergendoff visited their faculty in a style reminiscent of pastoral calls. Graceful and gracious, formal and personal, devout and scholarly, he modeled the good pastor. And the hospitable, outgoing, often irrepressible Gertrude Bergendoff—who knew everything about every student and staff member on campus, who thought "Dr. B." surpassed any speaker she had ever heard—epitomized the pastor's wife and helper. "She has carried more than her share of the responsibility in the president's home," Bergendoff said in his valedictory President's Report (1962), "and few are aware of the extent of her willing service."[5]

Dr. Bergendoff's interest in and sense of responsibility for his faculty's well-being, however, did not reach to interference in their work. Here strict professionalism prevailed; academic freedom was the inviolable rule. Choosing the best qualified instructors he could find, he left them alone to teach. "They knew their subjects; I didn't. What could I tell them about how to do their jobs?" he reflected in a conversation many years later (1985). More than one professor recalls being closely questioned by certain members of Augustana's Board of Directors about the conduct of administrative jobs or the contents of their courses, especially in positions related to student activities or courses in the sciences. An appeal to Dr. Bergendoff from professor or administrator inevitably produced the same reply: "How do you feel it should be done? That's how it will be done." Academic freedom reflected the liberating theology he embraced.

Conrad and Gertrude Bergendoff, on Conrad's eightieth birthday.
(Courtesy of Augustana College Library, Special Collections.)

Dr. Bergendoff has long been fascinated by the question of identity. "How do you know when you are you?" he asks. "At what age, at what state of development?" As far back as 1945 he was exploring this question. A college education, he suggested, should help form the "I," the identity, of each student by supplying the sense of direction that comes not just from knowledge, but from knowledge of and faith in God. "We are, and we are become, what we believe and what we hope," he told the graduating seniors in 1942.[6] This same question may well apply to the identity of an institution. In 1958, adapting Heraclitus, he used the metaphor of the Mississippi River, which flows just a mile or two to the north of the Rock Island campus, to describe the paradox of change and constancy that forms identity. "The stream that flows from the campus is always changing, as one generation follows another to generate power and give productiveness to the land. And though the campus will never hold just the same people again, the identity of Augustana will be kept clear."[7]

During the Bergendoff years (1935-1962) Augustana College and Theological Seminary experienced four major periods of change: the ebb of the war years, when men students went off to fight—many to die—and campus activities shrank to a thin but vigorous stream; then the post-war years, when returning veterans flooded the campus with their numbers and with agendas and behaviors that changed Augustana permanently; then the split between the college and seminary (1948), which looked to some like the "islanding" of Augustana College; and finally the 1950s, in many ways the "golden" years, when what Bergendoff had believed and hoped for had become Augustana, the current of its days and spirit swift and steady and strong. Now, in post-retirement, he not only watches from the shore but has stayed in the swim, enjoying a leadership of mind and spirit largely unchecked by the material exegencies of running a college. In each of these eras the vision he articulated has been "kept clear."

Edgar Carlson, a former student and colleague of Bergendoff, has noted several features of the latter's educational philosophy: Christian truth lies at the center of all learning; religion cannot be separated from knowledge because the Word of God is immanent in every academic discipline, and the faculty members of a Christian college are missionaries in their fields of thought.[8] Bergendoff had already demonstrated this philosophy during his years as Dean of the Seminary (1931-1935). According to Roald Tweet, Augustana professor of English and historian of the Bergendoff years, he recruited faculty members who insisted, in lecture and life, that theology meant action in the world, especially in issues of social justice.[9]

When Bergendoff assumed leadership of the college and seminary in 1936, he recognized that solid foundations had been laid "patiently, sacrificially, devotedly" by his predecessor Dr. Gustav Andreen for the kind of college they both wanted to build. Augustana was notable for academic ecumenicism. Though plagued by persistent financial difficulties, Andreen had managed, through patience, energy, and considerable charisma, to assemble a faculty of intellectual distinction as well as religious commitment. Dr. Henriette C. K. Naeseth demonstrated a University of Chicago-based precision and rigor in her literature courses. Dr. Fritiof M. Fryxell, himself an Augustana alumnus trained at the University of Chicago (and so highly esteemed that he was offered a teaching position there) returned to Augustana to create a department of geology in the heart and heat of the Scopes trial furor, asserting the college's faith in the validity of scientific inquiry—and the sturdiness of Christian doctrine to stand strong at the center of such inquiry. Depression strictures that threatened this promising educational program had been averted. When Augustana's science facilities were judged so inadequate by the North Central Colleges Association (of which Augustana was a charter member) that the Association threatened to rescind its accreditation, the Wallberg family came forward with funding for a new science building (1935). Under Martin Holcomb and Theodor LeVander, debate and oratory training replaced elocutionary techniques, and Holcomb established one of the country's first speech pathology instruction programs. Henry Veld had molded the separate Wennerberg (male) and Jenny Lind (female) choruses into a choir rapidly achieving national prominence.

After taking office Bergendoff initiated the practice of writing annual president's reports for the College and Seminary Board of Directors. These reports contain a detailed record of each year at the institutions, in both material and philosophical terms. They make fascinating reading. And they make it possible to trace the shape of Dr. Bergendoff's vision across the generations.[10]

Not surprisingly, from the beginning one theme emerges with persistent clarity: the college's connection with and support by the Church. Repeatedly Bergendoff stresses his "idea of a university." Church congregations must assume responsibility for the college and seminary that will ultimately produce their leaders, and this responsibility is twofold: to identify and encourage their ablest students to attend, and to contribute reliable financial support. Inadequate and erratic funding means neither faculty nor facilities can reach the excellence they must attain if the Church is to be served by the "highest type" of endeavor.

Conrad Bergendoff and Gustav Andreen, at about the time Bergendoff assumed office (1935). (Courtesy of Augustana College Library, Special Collections.)

Six years after Bergendoff took office, the thunder clouds of World War II threw their ominous shadows on this theme. With an estimated 12,000,000 men and women serving in the armed forces between 1940 and 1945, war efforts became a national preoccupation. Colleges and universities, full of service-age people, focused intensely on these efforts, especially after the bombing of Pearl Harbor in December 1941. "For every student the war has meant a radical change in outlook for the future," Bergendoff reported in 1942. "Daily chapel has reminded the students of those not here, for this year all the balcony has been vacant" (*PR*, 1942).

In 1995, drawing on both memory and his own reports from the time, he recalled:

> The educational world was shaken by what was happening, and produced many proposals [to address the situation]. Some leaders wanted to shorten college from four to three years, and lower standards for admission. Augustana resisted such changes. 'Indeed, we have believed that one of the accomplishments of higher education in wartime might be to keep calm and clear in the turmoil and confusion of the times.' The faculty [under Bergendoff's leadership] refused to lower standards for admission. It was ready to extend the summer courses so that a student could graduate in three years, though 'it is not sure that men going into the service of their country will be much concerned with the early possession of an A.B. degree.'[11]

Throughout this time, with steady vision and clear, measured rhetoric, Bergendoff held fast to his belief in the role of Christian higher education. Again and again, in daily chapel talks ("care is taken to make these brief moments as varied and profitable as possible"), in major addresses, in president's reports alike, Bergendoff insists that Augustana remember and uphold its central liberal arts curriculum.[12] "Cheapening of either education or the liberal arts degree is a dubious contribution to national welfare in this day, and Augustana's faith in education calls for just as high standards in wartime as in peace," he maintained (*PR*, 1942). And after the war? "None can foresee the eventual conflicts of ideas, ideals, customs, when the nations of the earth come in closer contact than ever before." His words suggest early recognition of the global village and the complex problems of an immediate physical accessibility not always matched by cross-cultural understanding. This vision of a changing world gave impetus to curricular review and revision at Augustana, not to weaken but to strengthen the liberal arts core, while the world "enter[ed] more deeply into the dark shadows of war" (*PR*, 1944).

An early advocate of "waging peace" in those dark years, Bergendoff demands yet more urgently that the Church, and therefore the church college, must engage in the world of political affairs. It must, as it has always done, serve radically to reshape that world. "Christian institutions of higher learning are the officers' training schools for the work of the Church in a post-war world"—and this work will be the revolution for peace by the "Truth which would turn the world upside down." To withdraw from the world, as some churches are doing, is to ignore the call of a God actively engaged in created reality. "It is the mission of the Church to locate and describe evil in high place and low, in government and in school, in social relationships and national policies," Bergendoff insists. We must not "narrow . . . the scope of revelation to a few documents, and restrict God's workings to Bible history."[13] He goes further: "I am terribly anxious about the ability of Christians to deceive themselves as to the nature and scope of their calling, their education, their use of time and treasure, talent and opportunity in the world."[14] Throughout his life he complemented rhetoric with action. He encouraged his faculty to work for social justice, and many of them spoke to such explosive issues as civil rights. Much later, Bergendoff's voice rose among the early protests against U. S. involvement in Viet Nam—a position for which he was both roundly vilified and warmly praised.

In 1943 the 68th College Training Detachment of the Army Air Corps—some 200 strong—arrived on campus for accelerated work that would qualify them as pilots, navigators, or bombardiers. Their presence in classrooms, dormitories, and in the nearby college drugstore, as well as their early Saturday morning drills and (sometimes) irreverent songs, brought the presence of the war vividly to the forefront of daily experience.[15]

By the spring semester of 1944, fifty men were in residence at the college, and eighty-one enrolled, as opposed to 322 women (339 male students had been on campus when Japan attacked Pearl Harbor). Long lists of Augustana students in uniform appeared in yearbooks and alumni bulletins. Starred names, indicating those lost in combat, multiplied. Special counseling services were established.

The painful war years, however, brought their own fruits. Bergendoff remembers that one result

was an expression of the faculty as to what should be a

graduate's preparation for the difficult years of peace, not less difficult than war years. It clarified the purpose of a Christian liberal arts college in a confused secular age. It did not propose to educate everybody. It did hope to influence leaders in every profession and stress the unity as well as the diversity of nations.[16]

Conrad Bergendoff during the World War II Years.
(Courtesy of Augustana College Library, Special Collections.)

Another effect of the war was an influx of highly qualified women students, many of whom profited from increased educational opportunities and went on to become distinguished scholars and teachers. One of them, Dr. Charlotte Erickson, was awarded a

MacArthur Fellowship in 1990, after concluding her teaching career with an appointment to a chair in history at Cambridge University, England—the first woman to be so designated by the university.

The dawn of peace broke on a dismantled world. Personal lives and political configurations alike had been broken. In the sphere of American education, one means of reassembling that world was the Servicemen's Readjustment Act of 1944, better known as the "G. I. Bill of Rights." More than 15,000,000 World War II veterans qualified for subsistence payments while attending college or training school, and the training institution received up to five hundred dollars a month for tuition, books, and fees for forty-eight months. Nearly 8,000,000 availed themselves of these benefits and comprised the "veteran bulge" that pushed college enrollments to an all-time high in 1947.[17] Each college or university was allowed to decide for itself whether or not to admit students who chose to attend under the provisions of the bill. Maintaining his conviction that Christian higher education must be actively engaged in the world, Bergendoff made the choice that altered the character of Augustana College: he admitted returning veterans on the G. I. Bill.

This step had far-reaching effects. Previously, students who attended Augustana had been a fairly homogeneous lot, drawn mainly from Lutheran Scandinavian-American immigrant families who wanted their children prepared for teaching and preaching. The returning veterans changed the complexion of the campus. They came with other ethnic identities, religious (or non-religious) affiliations, and other agendas; they wanted a place in the world they had fought to save, and that place was not necessarily in education or the ministry. They came, as one student from the mid-1940s recalls, "in flight jackets, pea jackets, army fatigues, carrying duffel bags, limping, strutting, smoking, cussing."[18] Nationally, college education was no longer an elitist privilege; locally, Augustana was no longer a Scandinavian-American enclave. A new era had begun.

In 1947, enrollment soared to an all-time high: 1,413 in the College, 212 in the School of Music. Facilities strained to accommodate the influx: "We were teaching in attics, closets, basements," one professor recalls. And new faculty, many from worlds very different from the Scandinavian-American community, were hired, lending strength and color to the current of college life.

Another factor changed the institution. In 1948, the Augustana Synod voted to separate college and seminary. Absent in Europe at the time, Bergendoff returned to find a *fait accompli* that appalled him.

Just the previous year he had noted, "I have sought to integrate the program of the college with the seminary." His President's Report of 1947-1948 contains some of his most powerful rhetoric; the anger of that time is caught in his words, in a syntax that coils and lashes:

> That it should fall to my lot to conclude this chapter of Augustana history was not imagined when I accepted the Synod call to become president in 1935 at an institution which had been one as long as the Synod itself. Every one of my predecessors—Esbjörn, Hasselquist, Olsson, Andreen—the men we honor this Centennial year [of the Augustana Lutheran Church]—had wrought and fought for the unity of the program of higher education. Convinced, as they were, that the progress of college and seminary went together and that the success of one aided the other, I have worked for 17 years to give outward expression to that idea that the Christian faith gives a wholeness of interpretation of the truth which no university can give except it confess that faith. . . . It was a testimony to an academic world all too split into unrelated parts, that our church believed that all truth is of God and all learning is related to the Word. . . .

And now, he says, "less than two years were needed to tear apart what had grown together for 86 years!" His disappointment is all the keener in that he finds no clear rationale for the split.

He objected on both philosophical and practical grounds: the split would weaken the seminary scholastically, and it would necessitate duplicating administrative costs. In all, he fears "that the children and grandchildren [will not be] able to maintain the vision their fathers had for Christian education" (PR, 1948).

The wisdom of the synodical action remains to be finally assessed. Surely it was taken at a time when no one on the Board could have predicted the demands on church and college from swiftly changing political and social realities, wide cultural diversity, and the critical need to address an increasingly accessible—but also increasingly fragmented world.

Whatever he might have felt about the "failure" of a seventeen-year goal, Bergendoff did not, however, surrender the vision. Convinced that "Augustana College means more to the church than any of us realizes," Bergendoff elected to head the college rather than the seminary when offered the choice.

It was a move that astonished some onlookers in the Augustana Synod. The seminary presidency was then deemed the more "prestigious" position; after all, Augustana College had been formed originally for the purpose of bringing students up to speed for their studies in the ministry. But in fact the choice was natural for Bergendoff, nor should it have surprised anyone who had been listening carefully to his ideas of education. In his letter to the Seminary Board he stated that he had tried to create a wholeness of educational experience that included both college and seminary; and, viewing the decision to split the two as a mandate for change, he did not know what "different" course he would pursue with the seminary. Therefore he relinquished its leadership. Of his vision for the college he had no doubt.

*

Recently, at the age of 99, Dr. Bergendoff described watching Augustana students process across snow-covered fields to the Jenny Lind Chapel in nearby Andover, Illinois, where L. P. Esbjörn, Augustana's first president, had established his first American parish. The sight of the young people, bundled in winter coats, walking in a long line, and carrying tapers to light their way to the candlelit chapel where communion was being served, was, Dr. Bergendoff said, "an inspiration in itself." The picture that deeply moved him is paradigmatic of the function he saw the college fulfilling: sending young people out into a dark world, holding candles against the night. If in 1948 the "university" he had dreamed of was eclipsed, still the college he headed could be a mission field of the Church, asserting the wholeness of God's kingdom to a world in need of healing. "How do you know when you are you?" Perhaps his sense that identity is flexible aided him in rethinking the place of Augustana College. At any rate, he wasted little time in unproductive regrets. And during the 1950s the college of his dream took shape.

In 1955, looking back over the twenty years of his presidency, Bergendoff recapitulated the goals he had formed in 1935. Most of them had been achieved or were in the process of being realized: an endowment fund had increased from $923,018 to $2,500,000; Andreen Hall was built to house 200 male students; a new Fine Arts Building was scheduled to open in September 1955, with a complementary 1,600-seat auditorium to complete the Fine Arts complex five years later; a library of 90,000 volumes was in place; and a unified campus landscape plan was taking shape. The student body had grown from 511 to 1,103, and faculty members had doubled to keep pace. During mid-fifties prosperity he rejoiced in the possibilities for expansion—an increasing population promised an enlarged pool of prospective students—but he also remembered the need for and the costs of providing adequate facilities to maintain educational excellence.

Affirmations of that excellence continued to mount throughout the decade: a Phi Beta Kappa chapter was established in 1949, the American Chemical Society accredited Augustana in 1955, the Augustana Choir appeared on national television (1952) and marked the quarter-century anniversary of its first appearance in Chicago's Orchestra Hall with a gala reception at the Congress Hotel following a 1956 concert there. Honors accumulated for the oratory and debate programs, with individuals and teams placing high in state and national contests. Augustana was the only school that had qualified for the West Point Invitational Debate Tournament every year since the contest had been established. A consultant in higher education hired by the Augustana Lutheran Church to evaluate its five colleges praised Augustana as "one of the outstanding liberal arts and church colleges . . . The [Lutheran Church has] been significantly influenced through leaders from the alumni of Augustana College." Galesburg poet Carl Sandburg, honorary alumnus, put it more informally in a 1957 letter to Bergendoff: "Admiring your report for the academic year '56-'57 I had to say, 'Good and beneficent Lord, what would that grand old pioneer [T. N.] Hasselquist [second president of Augustana] say of the seed sown long ago?'"

Fullbrights, Guggenheims, National Science Foundation awards supported faculty research, and Bergendoff noted with satisfaction that a small overturn, despite more lucrative offers elsewhere, demonstrated that this faculty was committed to the ideal of education for which Augustana stood. Students came with strong records, scored above average on national tests, and left with fellowships and grants to attend graduate schools nationwide. On campus they are "a healthy, hopeful, earnest, and eager group," according to then-Dean of Women Betsey Brodahl. "I don't know where a finer group of a thousand young people would be found," Dr. Bergendoff said. "Cynics and pessimists might change their attitude if they associated more with them" (PR, 1952).

College and community relationships broadened and deepened with the expansion of the Foundation for Crippled Children and Adults (later the Easter Seal Foundation), and with opportunities provided by the Handel Oratorio Society, a town and gown performance series, and the many campus cultural events open to the public.

Conrad Bergendoff at Augustana's Baccalaureate, 1972.
(Courtesy of Augustana College Library, Special Collections.)

Looking ahead to the centennial year, 1960, gave fresh energy and impetus to college plans for expansion, since the Church was to hold its Centennial Convention in Rock Island. Bergendoff dreamed of a well maintained, beautified campus. Already in 1957 1,354 trees in forty-five varieties grew there. "Who can estimate the silent influence a beautiful campus can make on the hundreds of young people who daily walk over it? This, too, is part of an education," Bergendoff believed. But as he planned for change, he also stressed continuity:

> ... We have considered the college as an institution minister-
> ing in the field of education to all who would wish to benefit
> by such a ministry. ... After a century we count it a favorable
> situation to have over a dozen different denominations
> represented in our student body. ... We ask both of students
> and faculty respect for the avowed purpose of the school, but
> we do not proselytize anyone. If the Lutheran position has any
> merit, it should be proved in spirit and in deed. ... We try to
> make it clear that we believe higher education should include
> knowledge and reverence for man's spiritual heritage—his
> most significant possession—and that worship is part of any
> cultured person's life (*PR*, 1959).

In the face of late-fifties' national "crash programs" in math and
science, engendered by fear of Russian technological supremacy,
Bergendoff insisted, as he also had done during the war years, on the
liberal arts balance: "We need engineers, but we also need men and
women to decide what use shall be made of weapons of war" (*PR*,
1959). His final President's Report, issued in 1962, is entitled *The Idea
of a Christian College* and contains his assessment of Augustana's goals
and successes in reaching them. Echoes of his inaugural address
sound in the words: "The glory of the church college is that it has
freedom to acknowledge the dominion of Christ, and to employ this
freedom from human slaveries—of body and of mind—in the arts
and sciences, in religion and philosophy, in learning and in living."

Bergendoff's valedictory analysis of what the Christian college
should be about, supplied the agenda for his own life. In post-
retirement years, now more numerous than the years of his presidency, he has remained in the community of the Quad-Cities, variously
honored by that community. In 1988, for instance, his ninety-third
birthday was declared "Dr. Conrad Bergendoff day" by the four cities
that comprise the two-state area (a rare instance of concord among
the cities!). He has watched faculty members he hired reach distinction in their careers. One of them, Augustana alumna Dr. Dorothy
Parkander, occupies the first fully-endowed academic chair in the
college's history, significantly named the Conrad Bergendoff Chair in
the Humanities. He has watched his faculty complete careers. Many
of them he has buried. His continuing zeal for Augustana's welfare
has rallied the loyalty of college and alumni alike. And he vigorously

incarnates the ideal he articulated back in 1936, continuing to engage in and with a changing world. His interests range widely—from politics to ecology (until a few years ago he was an avid hiker), to music and art (he attends most of the concerts and gallery shows at the college), to church and college history. He reads omnivorously, in several languages. He wonders; he questions; he writes. And more than when the dignity of his presidential office conferred a certain formality on his behavior, he teases and laughs.

*

Until a few years ago we walked, spring and fall, through Black Hawk Park, a local forest preserve he loves and helped save from the developers' bulldozer. Woody paths twist through stands of wild-flowers, over creeks, along river bluffs. We talk, and we sit and are silent. Sometimes he reaches for my shoulder to steady himself. I remember that time years ago when his hands steadied me in the Augustana swimming pool. He speaks of the wonder of a breaking trillium, of a flaming leaf, of a cardinal's song, of the small sounds of water that thread around us. He speaks of the strength and complexity of silence. And like many others before me, I feel how then and now his words steady the world around him.

NOTES

[1] Conrad Bergendoff, "Dr. Bergendoff's Inaugural Address," *Augustana Observer*, 1 October 1936, 4.
[2] *Ibid.*
[3] Conrad Bergendoff, *President's Report*, Augustana College, 1946.
[4] Paper delivered at Conference of Lutheran Theological Faculties, Philadelphia, 1946.
[5] *The Idea of a Christian College* (President's Report, Augustana College), 1962.
[6] Baccalaureate Sermon, Augustana College, 1942.
[7] *President's Report*, Augustana College, 1958.
[8] Edgar Carlson, "Dr. Bergendoff and His Contribution to the Church and Christian Higher Education," *The Immigrant Community in Transition: Essays in Honor of Dr. Conrad Bergendoff*, ed. J. Iverne Dowie and Ernest M. Espelie, Rock Island, Illinois: Augustana Historical Society, 1963.
[9] See, for example, his eulogy to A. D. Mattson, delivered at St. John's Lutheran Church, Rock Island, in October 1970. He praises Mattson for awakening the social conscience of the Augustana Synod.
[10] All subsequent quotations from these reports will be cited in the text as *PR*, with the appropriate year.
[11] "The College and the War," *Augustana College Magazine*, Summer 1995.

[12] Bergendoff's insistence on the importance of liberal arts did not preclude adding courses that served specific needs of the war effort. Spherical trigonometry, conservation of natural resources, economics of war and defense, industrial chemical calculations, industrial chemistry, America at war, Red Cross first aid, home nursing and hygiene, as well as elementary nutrition and household economy, all recommended by the National Defense Council, were added during 1941-1942.

[13] Paper delivered at Conference of Lutheran Theological Faculties.

[14] Baccalaureate Sermon, Augustana College, 1945.

[15] Richard B. Powers, "The U. S. Army Air Corps' Invasion of Augustana," *Augustana College Magazine*, Summer 1995.

[16] "The College and the War."

[17] United States, Office of Public Affairs, "Talking Points: 50th Anniversary of the GI Bill," March 1994.

[18] Quoted by Betsey Brodahl, professor emerita of history, Augustana College.

CONRAD BERGENDOFF AND THE LCA MERGER OF 1962[1]

MARK A. GRANQUIST

The history of American Lutheranism in the twentieth century has been dominated to a great extent by three periods of institutional or denominational merger, with the remaining time devoted to merger negotiations, or working through the effects of mergers.[2] This is not to say that negotiations and mergers were the only important developments; the growth of American Lutheranism in this century has been dramatic in many ways. But the rounds of institutional change have been vitally important, not only in regard to the structural shape of American Lutheranism, but also to the ways in which these Lutheran groups have grown and developed. Decisions that were made in the course of these negotiations have had implications that reached far beyond their limited settings. As a theologian and institutional leader within the Augustana Lutheran Church, Dr. Conrad Bergendoff participated in a number of these merger negotiations, and his voice was distinct and influential in its support of unity. This paper will examine the role played by Bergendoff in the merger negotiations that eventually produced the Lutheran Church in America (1962-1988), and his wider influence on the movement for Lutheran unity, especially in the 1950s.

This narrative actually extends back to 1918, when Bergendoff, then a ministerial student at the Lutheran Theological Seminary at Philadelphia, was an observer at the convention that brought the United Lutheran Church in America (1918-1962) into existence. The ULCA was composed of three groups of Lutherans that had their roots in the Eastern states, dating back to Colonial America. The Augustana Lutheran Church had joined one of these groups, the General Council, as a federated member but in 1918 decided not to follow the rest of the General Council into the ULCA merger. Bergendoff sent a report back from the New York convention for the English-language Augustana periodical *Lutheran Companion*, describing the scene in glowing detail—and leaving no doubt that he felt that Augustana should not have abandoned the General Council.

Looking ahead, Bergendoff viewed this merger as only a beginning:

> The United Lutheran Church would go about its work, the
> other synods about theirs, all looking for the day when identity
> of interests and identity of work would bring all Lutheran
> synods together, when even this United Church would merge
> itself into the larger Church—a truly United Lutheran Church
> in America.[3]

Given these sentiments, it is clear that Bergendoff's choice for the
union of all American Lutherans was made at a very early date. This
appreciation of the ULCA also was to become evident during the
tortuous merger negotiations of the 1950s.

After the end of the first round of mergers, somewhere about
1930, the field of American Lutheran groups had been narrowed to
ten major denominations, along with two significant federative bodies
(see Table 1). The ULCA anchored one end of this spectrum; the
other end was dominated by the Evangelical Lutheran Synod of
Missouri and Other States (later the Lutheran Church-Missouri
Synod). Between these two were various groups of Midwestern-based
Scandinavian and German Lutherans. Bergendoff's Augustana Synod
was here, as were the United Norwegian Lutheran Church, the
American Lutheran Church (1930-60), and smaller groups of Danes
and Finns. These Midwestern groups cooperated in a federative body,
the American Lutheran Conference (1930-54), which, with the
addition of the ULCA, constituted the National Lutheran Council
(1918-1966).

There were significant tensions within the center of American
Lutheranism— mainly the Midwestern groups comprising the
American Lutheran Council—over the direction and standards for
future Lutheran unity after 1930. Although there were those with
differing opinions within each denomination, the overall tendency of
each group was fairly clear. With its historic ties to the General
Council, the Augustana Synod would resist any attempt to exclude
the ULCA from future plans; the United Norwegian Lutheran Church
and the American Lutheran Church were oriented more toward
Missouri. The fault line was this reality: it was seen as difficult or
impossible at the time to design negotiations that would include both
the ULCA *and* Missouri. If the Midwesterners in the American
Lutheran Conference were to look beyond themselves for merger
partners, either the ULCA or Missouri would be excluded. This basic

TABLE 1

INSTITUTIONAL STRUCTURES OF AMERICAN LUTHERANS
1900-1960 ++

*United Lutheran Church in America (1918-62)
Eastern German Lutherans from colonial times -- merged in 1918

American
Lutheran   *Augustana Evangelical Lutheran Church
Conference   (1860-1962) Swedish
(cooperative
   body, 1930-54)   *Evangelical Lutheran Church (1917-60)
                  Norwegian—merger of various Norwegian groups

                              *United Evangelical Lutheran Church
                                        (1896-1960) Danish

                              *Lutheran Free Church (1897-1963)
                                              Norwegian

                              *American Lutheran Church (1930-60)
                              German—merger of some midwestern
                                        German Lutheran groups

---

Lutheran Church-Missouri Synod (1847-)
German; conservative confessional midwest Lutheran group

* Members of the National Lutheran Council (1918-66)—a cooperative
body that included ULCA and churches of the American Lutheran
Conference, but not Missouri.

++ Note that denominational names change over time; each name
given is the last given name of that particular group.

tension existed until the separate merger negotiations that produced the two new Lutheran denominations in the early 1960s. The Augustana Synod had its feet in two separate camps, as a part of the American Lutheran Conference, and as an historic friend of the ULCA.

It is significant, however, that Bergendoff himself came into these American Lutheran merger negotiations from a different perspective, as his first ecumenical experiences were at the international level. During 1926-27, Bergendoff was a graduate student in Europe, where he worked with Swedish Archbishop Nathan Söderblom on projects including a conference to continue the focus and dialogue of the 1925 Stockholm Conference on Life and Work. Bergendoff attended the Second World Conference on Faith and Order in Edinburgh in 1937 as an official representative of the Augustana Synod and was named to that Conference's Continuation Committee.[4] He also participated as an official representative of the Synod to the Third World Conference on Faith and Order in Lund in 1952, the Lutheran World Federation conventions in Lund (1947), Hannover (1952), and Minneapolis (1957), the National Council of Churches Convention in Cleveland (1950), and the World Council of Churches meeting in Evanston (1954).[5] These national and international ecumenical experiences gave Bergendoff a broad perspective from which to view the questions of Lutheran merger and unity. One is struck by both his vision, and sometimes his impatience, with the often murky progress of inter-Lutheran negotiations.

From its beginnings in 1930, the American Lutheran Conference was seen as a vehicle for further Lutheran merger negotiations, but with the faults and tensions outlined above. There were many difficulties involved in these unity discussions, some practical and social, others theological. The most important question, however, could be neatly phrased: "How much unity is needed as a basis for Lutheran union?" Some held a narrow view, insisting on complete resolution of all theological issues before a merger could take place. This perspective was also suspicious of the Lutheran "credentials" of some Lutheran groups (most notably the ULCA). Others in the Conference maintained a broader position, feeling that it was enough to agree on the essentials of Lutheranism, and that the proclaimed Lutheran identity of any group should be trusted.

Bergendoff was in the latter camp, and publicized his view in a number of articles in the late 1930s. In an article on the relation of the American Lutheran Conference to the ULCA in 1937, Bergendoff attempted to find some middle ground that could bring the two groups closer together.[6] He also challenged what he perceived to be the narrowness of certain Lutheran groups, especially the Missouri Synod, in an article in 1939, saying:

> I question the method of attaining fellowship which consists in one party offering a document to the other to be signed on the dotted line. . . . we are to meet each other as Lutherans, and not as supplicants asking for the right to be called Lutheran by others who have decided what Lutheranism is.[7]

Bergendoff also published a number of articles in the *Journal of the American Lutheran Conference*, including one in 1943 entitled "American Lutherans and the Doctrine of the Church," striking a soon-to-be-familiar theme, a plea for an inclusive vision for American Lutherans.[8] This was a theme that he would expand upon during the negotiations of the 1950s.

During the 1940s, the American Lutheran Conference was the center of merger talks and activities. The question, however, still was: how wide the door, and who would be invited to talk? When the Conference met in Rock Island in November 1942, it had before it a resolution calling for negotiations of the broadest sort, a resolution largely the creation of Augustana Synod leaders, including Bergendoff. More specifically, the resolution called for the Executive Committee to "negotiate with all other Lutheran bodies, looking toward a more inclusive organization." The resolution also contained a sentence, authored by Bergendoff, that stated:

> As a necessary step to this end this Conference urges its constituent members to invite into pulpit and altar fellowship those Lutheran groups with whom they are not now in fellowship.[9]

Bergendoff was urging not only eventual merger, but interim steps to recognize the "Lutheran-ness" of other Lutheran denominations. This resolution set in motion a long and complex series of negotiations that were to result in merger talks beginning in 1949.

In 1943, Bergendoff convened in Rock Island the first conference for American Lutheran professors of theology, a meeting that brought together scholars from the whole spectrum of American Lutheranism: the Missouri Synod, the American Lutheran Conference, and the

ULCA.[10] The conference was an attempt to get the theologians of the various denominations together to discuss common issues. The results of the conference were finally published in 1947, and predictably, Bergendoff's contribution was an essay on "Lutheran Unity." Though this essay is largely historical, Bergendoff did raise some familiar issues, at one point asking rhetorically:

> Why all the constant search of Lutherans for formulae of agreement among themselves? Do the Lutheran bodies not, by their very uneasiness in isolation, proclaim that the Lord wills that such unity as exists shall be made evident?[11]

Though this conference and subsequent meetings were well attended, this group did not lead the way to greater unity. To demonstrate the depth of the problem, Bergendoff even had to worry whether his arrangements for worship at the conference would offend the Missouri delegates.[12]

In 1948, the continual urging for closer cooperation and possible union among the members of the American Lutheran Conference was renewed, and it was decided that representatives of all the Lutheran groups in the National Lutheran Conference (which included ULCA but not Missouri) would meet in January 1949 to discuss future steps toward unity. These representatives, the so-called "Committee of Thirty-Four," eventually issued a resolution calling for negotiations on structural union to be conducted within the framework of the National Lutheran Council. That this was unanimously passed, however, is not to obscure that the ALC and the United Norwegians had serious reservations about the inclusion of the ULCA in these talks. As a parallel to these negotiations, then, the Norwegians, the ALC, and a Danish group formed a Joint Committee on Union in 1949, which sought a smaller union of Lutheran bodies within the American Lutheran Conference. This union was to take place on the basis of several doctrinal statements from earlier negotiations, statements that would effectively remove the ULCA from any negotiations.[13]

These events left the Augustana Synod in a quandary: should it push for the larger union within the National Lutheran Council or join the smaller movement to unite with the American Lutheran Conference? The Augustana Synod had partisans on both sides of the issue; some wished to maintain ties with the rest of the American Lutheran Conference groups, even if this meant the exclusion of the

ULCA, while others saw the principle of wider Lutheran unity as being of paramount importance. Bergendoff was clearly in the latter group.[14]

As a basis for merger negotiations, the Joint Committee on Union developed a document entitled "United Testimony on Faith and Life," based on older doctrinal statements. The "United Testimony" reflected a fairly narrow view of Lutheran unity that demanded substantial doctrinal agreement beyond the Lutheran confessions before fellowship or merger could proceed. This approach to Lutheran union, and the practical questions of how to proceed, were the main topics of discussion for the Augustana Synod when it met in convention in Des Moines in June 1952.

Bergendoff was a leader of those who opposed the "United Testimony," and he argued vigorously against it in a speech to the convention. Suggesting that the "United Testimony" was inadequate and unnecessary as a basis for a merger, Bergendoff stated:

> It is a fallacy of unity negotiations that we have to prove that we *are* Lutherans. . . We are never going to get anywhere in any unity negotiations if we must rewrite the confessional books of the Lutheran Church. What we must try to do is to get Lutherans to recognize Lutherans.[15]

This view of unity prevailed at the convention, which passed a resolution committing itself to a wider and more inclusive merger than the one envisioned by the Joint Committee on Union. At this convention, too, the Synod selected a Committee on Lutheran Unity to represent Augustana at any future merger negotiations; and Bergendoff was appointed as one of its members.[16] This Augustana Committee met with the Joint Committee on Union in November 1952; but the Joint Committee would not open negotiations with the ULCA, and thus the Augustana delegates walked out of the meeting. Augustana would no longer be a part of the merger of the American Lutheran Conference churches.

During this time, Bergendoff was writing a number of items that expanded his views on the doctrine of the Church and on his view of unity. In a 1952 article in the *Lutheran Companion* he observed:

> ". . . we are dealing not with *our* unity, but with the unity of the *Church*. . . The Church is greater than any of our synods, but unfortunately our high sounding names, as Churches,

make us believe that it is ours to order all the affairs of the Church. . . All American Lutheran groups are but synods . . . We are parts of the Lutheran Church in America, and no one part is as great as the whole.[17]

Bergendoff expanded on this theme in 1953, when he delivered the Hoover Lectures on Christian Unity at the University of Chicago, addressing the theme of the "One, Holy, Catholic, and Apostolic Church." These lectures, later published under the same title, addressed the implications of this phrase from the Nicene Creed for Christian unity. Arguing that the unity of the churches is more a matter of spirit than of organization, Bergendoff continued:

No member of the body of Christ lives to himself. Whether we acknowledge it or not, incorporation into His body places us into relation to all the others in the body, and no denial of fellowship on our part can rend the unity of the Body—it can only separate us from the fullness of grace dwelling in the integration of the members in unity.[18]

Taking this idea further in a 1954 article, Bergendoff suggested that there already was a deep unity of faith among Lutherans in America, but then challenged other church leaders:

Theirs is a grave responsibility who would place the regulations of men in the way of access to the Lord's table . . . our own Church is not free of the temptation to confuse the ordinances of men with the ordinances of God.[19]

Bergendoff allows that there are times when it is necessary to remain separate to "guard the truth of the faith," but reminds his readers that truth is ultimately Christ's alone.

On 10 November 1954, the American Lutheran Conference was dissolved, its role now past. For the following two days, 11-12 November, there was a Lutheran Free Conference that involved many of the same delegates. This conference was hoped to stimulate ideas toward unity, but it came to no conclusions. On 15 November, the Augustana Commission on Ecumenical Relations[20] convened, attempting to set up further inter-denominational meetings and to determine more precisely the essential conditions for Lutheran unity. Bergendoff was selected as a member of a study committee to explore this latter issue.[21] Throughout 1955, Augustana and the ULCA sought to pull other Lutheran groups into further negotiations, a strategy that culminated in Augustana and the ULCA inviting fourteen other groups to join them in further negotiations. Many of the other Lutheran bodies rejected the call, but favorable responses were received from the Finnish Evangelical Lutheran Church (Suomi Synod) and the American Evangelical Lutheran Church (one of the Danish Lutheran bodies). These four groups met on 12 December 1956 in Chicago to form the Joint Commission on Lutheran Unity (JCLU). This commission would begin the negotiations that would lead directly to the formation of the Lutheran Church in America in 1962.

Throughout 1955 and 1956, Bergendoff kept up his written offensive for Lutheran unity. In an article in 1955, he expressed his fear that the formation of two or three larger Lutheran denominations might actually retard the push toward unity: "Powerful Lutheran Churches opposed to each other may be a greater disaster than weak Lutheran synods overlapping each other."[22] In 1955 he addressed the topic, "Augustana's Idea of the Church" in the Alumni Lectures at Augustana Theological Seminary,[23] and presented a paper to the Lutheran World Federation entitled, "Our Oneness in Christ and Our Disunity as Churches."[24] Finally, in 1956 Bergendoff presented the ULCA's Knubel-Miller Lectures, on the topic, "The Doctrine of the Church in American Lutheranism," lectures that were eventually printed under this title.[25]

When the Joint Commission on Lutheran Unity (JCLU) met for the first time in December 1956, Bergendoff was one of the official representatives of the Augustana Lutheran Church. At that first meeting Bergendoff read a paper on "The Lutheran Doctrine of the Church," a form of his published Knubel-Miller lectures.[26] This paper was highly influential in the proceedings: the Commission adopted a motion that a copy of the paper itself be provided to each of its members.[27] The basic problem facing the Commission was with the differing systems of governance in the merging churches; the ULCA was essentially a federation of synods (or intermediate judicatories), whereas in the other three groups, power was more strongly concentrated in the national church organizations.[28] Bergendoff's vision of the nature of the Church seemed to have influenced the JCLU to accept a broader role for the national church entity. One participant in the JCLU reflected later that Bergendoff was one of those on the commission "most respected for his wisdom,"[29] and in this case the JCLU seemed to follow his lead.

In a later matter, however, Bergendoff threw the JCLU into a quandary. This was over the matter of "lodges," an issue with some history among American Lutherans. The question was whether Lutherans, especially Lutheran ministers, could hold memberships in lodges or secret societies such as the Masons. More conservative Lutherans thought this unacceptable, while the ULCA took a less rigid view; the differences had been a bone of contention. At the JCLU meeting of 18 September 1957, while the commission was discussing the qualifications for ministers, Bergendoff submitted a "Recommendation in re: Qualifications of Ministers," that stated:

A candidate shall not be ordained into the ministry of this Church who is pledged to loyalty to any organization—secret or public—which practices religious observances not in full conformity with his witness to Christ as defined in the Lutheran Confessions. Nor may anyone ordained into the ministry of this Church pledge such loyalty subsequent to his ordination. . . .[30]

This threw the meeting into an uproar, for such language was unacceptable to the ULCA. Action on the Recommendation was deferred until the Commission's meeting in December.

According to one participant, the discussions on the issue in the December meeting were "warm" and "lengthy."[31] Numerous attempts were made by ULCA delegates to amend the Recommendation, or to substitute other motions, but all of these attempts were defeated by the JCLU as a whole. As Bergendoff later recalled:

In retrospect I view the episode as critical in the negotiations—indeed it might have been the occasion for the failure of the proposed merger. . . . There is no reason to recall the discussion except to emphasize that we had reached the stage where Augustana, for all its interest in merger, was ready to break off.[32]

At this point the ULCA delegates withdrew into a caucus to discuss the issue among themselves. Their leader, the ULCA President Franklin Clark Fry, returned ten minutes later to announce that the delegation would cede the issue, and made the vote unanimous for the Augustana position.[33] This was perhaps one of the most crucial moments in the entire negotiations, but it passed safely.

As the work of the JCLU moved into building the organizational structure of the new Church, Bergendoff seems to have had little responsibility. He was not listed as a member of any of the various committees developed to explore the areas of formation.[34] When the Augustana leadership met in conference on 14-16 January 1959 to discuss the progress of negotiations, Bergendoff gave a report on "Worship," which simply informed the meeting that a Commission on Worship was being planned.[35] But in February 1959, Franklin Clark Fry gave Bergendoff the important assignment of drafting the preamble to the Constitution of the new church. The first draft, dated 20 February 1959, was submitted to the JCLU at its meeting on 5 March 1959.[36] One participant recalled,

> . . . the Commission waited with this main introduction. Then it turned the task over to Conrad Bergendoff, who was trusted to say the right things; he came up with a beautiful and profound statement. He was nudged here and there by Franklin Clark Fry so as to conform with the right preamble technique.[37]

This preamble, or course, went through a number of drafts before it was included in the Constitution of the Lutheran Church in America.

Though the merger negotiations were progressing well by this point, other duties remained. One important task was to explain the merger to the Augustana Synod itself, and to convince synodical delegates to approve it. Though the majority of the Synod seemed to favor the merger, there were also voices raised against this action. Some urged that it was not too late to abandon these talks and to enter into the Joint Commission on Unity negotiations.[38] At the Synod Convention of 1959, the Commission on Ecumenical Relations presented a report that explained the progress achieved thus far and urged the Synod finally to adopt the merger when the negotiations were completed.[39]

The year 1960 was pivotal in the history of Augustana, as the initial vote was taken in convention to ratify the merger. It was also the year of the Synod's centennial and was thus a time of looking both to the past and to the future. In a speech at the Centennial service in June of 1960, Bergendoff addressed this matter:

The willingness of the Augustana Church to give up its identity after one hundred years of fruitful activity is itself an evidence of a faith that the future will be different from the past. We are not laying down our tools because the work is done. We are rather taking up new tools for the greater task ahead.[40]

He suggested that the task facing the new church in 1960 was as difficult (if not more difficult) than the task that faced the founders of the Augustana Synod in 1860.

Even as the finishing touches were being put on the merger negotiations in 1960, there were new currents of negotiation that would expand the cooperative efforts of American Lutherans. The question involved the National Lutheran Council and its future. Founded in 1918, the NLC gained strength and responsibilities during the 1940s and 1950s. But what would happen to the NLC after the two mergers were completed—would it have any place or function? After a long series of efforts, and after a significant commitment by the President of the Lutheran Church-Missouri Synod, delegates of the NLC and the Missouri Synod met in Chicago in July 1960 to talk about future arrangements and cooperation. These talks were the beginning of a process that would lead to the formation in 1966 of the Lutheran Council in the USA, a cooperative organization that would include 95 percent of American Lutherans, including the Missouri Synod.[41]

Bergendoff was a representative of the National Lutheran Council during these negotiations, and he played a characteristic role. At the initial meeting he was selected to deliver a paper entitled, "A Lutheran Study of Church Unity," in tandem with a theologian of the Missouri Synod, Dr. Martin Franzmann. Bergendoff set the tone for the meeting with his assertion,

Confessional Agreement is sufficient for participation in the kinds of task undertaken by the National Lutheran Council and this cooperation is a witness to an existing unity in doctrine which finds expression in practice.[42]

Later these two papers were printed by the NLC and the Missouri Synod. In his address to these discussions, Bergendoff suggested that substantial unity already existed between these groups, and that it was their task to discover their unity. Furthermore, he added,

The proposition of complete unity or none at all cannot be defended. . . . Rather the Scriptures teach a unity between the believer and the Redeemer which issues in a unity between believers that varies according to circumstances. It is the continuing task of the church to identify the unity that exists...[43]

The negotiations to form LCUSA moved slowly, but the goal was eventually reached.

There was one final way in which Bergendoff contributed to the formation of the Lutheran Church in America, and that was by becoming the first Executive Secretary of the LCA Board of Theological Education. Bergendoff had a long and vital interest in education, specifically theological education. He fought (but lost) the decision in 1948 to separate Augustana Theological Seminary from Augustana College, the academic institution he continued to serve as President until 1962. With the formation of the LCA in 1962, Bergendoff was persuaded to accept the position of Executive Secretary by Franklin Clark Fry.[44] Bergendoff accepted this assignment with the understanding that he and the Board would launch a systematic study of theological education in the new Church.[45] This study resulted in a report to the 1964 LCA convention, a document popularly referred to as the "Bergendoff Report."[46] The report itself was blunt in its assessment of the seminaries of the new church—there were too many, they were underfunded, and academic standards were weak. The report called for four consolidated institutions in various geographical areas of the country. As one historian commented, "Needless to say, some peoples' favorite oxen were gored in the process."[47] Some of the elements of the plan were adopted, such as the formation of the Lutheran School of Theology at Chicago, but other elements, such as the merger of the Philadelphia and Gettysburg seminaries, were scuttled by vested interests.

To conclude this study, a few general observations are in order. It is clear that Bergendoff was a key participant in the negotiations that produced the Lutheran Church in American in 1962. His vision of an open and inclusive merger process led him to push Augustana away from the American Lutheran Conference negotiations (JCU) in the early 1950s, standing by the principle of inclusion of the ULCA. Bergendoff was an active participant in the JCLU negotiations that produced the Lutheran Church in American in 1962. He made important contributions at critical junctures in the process of negotiations, steering the Augustana Lutheran Church into the JCLU talks and into acceptance of the results. And as the first Executive Secretary for LCA Board of Theological Education, he struggled to strengthen seminary education in the new church.

Yet his influence on the process was larger than this, in his long-standing vision and commitment to unity, not only among American Lutherans, but among Christians around the world. From an early age he had a vision of the unity of the Church that transcended lines of denomination and communion, a unity in Christ that was waiting to be discovered by Christians of various persuasions. His vision of 1918, of a "truly United Lutheran Church in America" is still to be attained, but his efforts from the 1930s through the 1960s played a significant role in bringing this reality closer to fruition.

NOTES

[1] The author would like to thank Mr. Chester Johnson of the Archives of Gustavus Adolphus College, Saint Peter, Minnesota, for his kind assistance with the research for this article.

[2] The first period of merger was from 1917 to 1930, which saw the formation of the United Norwegian Lutheran Church (1917-1960), the United Lutheran Church in America (1918-1962), and the old American Lutheran Church (1930-1960), along with the formation of two collaborative bodies, the National Lutheran Council (1918-1966) and the American Lutheran Conference (1930-1954). The second period began in the late 1940s, and saw the formation of the American Lutheran Church (1960-1988) and the Lutheran Church of America (1962-1988), along with a new collaborative body, the Lutheran Council in the USA (1966-1988). The third round began in the late 1960s, and culminated in the formation of the Evangelical Lutheran Church in America (1988-). For the history of these mergers and negotiations see E. Clifford Nelson, *Lutheranism in North America, 1914-1970*, Minneapolis: Augsburg Publishing House, 1972, and Edward C. Fendt, *The Struggle for Lutheran Unity and Consolidation in the U.S.A. from the Late 1930's to the Early 1970's*, Minneapolis: Augsburg Publishing House, 1980.

[3] "Impressions from the 'Merger Meeting' in New York City, Nov. 12-18, 1918," *Lutheran Companion*, 26, 7 December 1918, pp. 627-28.

[4] For this, see Dorris A. Flessner, *American Lutherans Help Shape the World Council: the role of the Lutheran Churches of America in the Formation of the World Council of Churches*, n.p.: Lutheran Historical Conference, 1981, pp. 17-19.

[5] On these involvements, see G. Everett Arden, *Augustana Heritage*, Rock Island: Augustana Press, 1963, especially pp. 297-311.

[6] "The Relationship Between the American Lutheran Conference and the United Lutheran Church in America," *Augustana Quarterly*, 16, October, 1937, pp. 318-29.

[7] "Here We Stand! The Teachings and Practices of the Augustana Synod," *Lutheran Companion*, 47, 30 March 1939, pp. 329-93.

[8] "American Lutherans and the Doctrine of the Church," *Lutheran Outlook*, 8, May, 1943, 83-84. Also from this period of time was his book, *I Believe in the Church*, Rock Island:

Augustana Book Concern, 1937, and "The True Unity of the Church," *Lutheran Church Quarterly*, 12, July, 1939, pp. 257-77; this last was Bergendoff's Holman lectures at the Lutheran Theological Seminary at Gettysburg.

[9] Cited in Nelson, *Lutheranism in North America*, p. 170.

[10] Fendt, *The Struggle for Lutheran Unity*, p. 23.

[11] "Lutheran Unity," in E.C. Fendt, ed, *What Lutherans Are Thinking: A Symposium on Lutheran Faith and Life*, Columbus: Wartburg Press, 1947, p. 386.

[12] Fendt, *The Struggle for Lutheran Unity*, p. 26.

[13] On these negotiations, see Nelson, *Lutheranism in North America*, pp. 175-80, and Arden, *Augustana Heritage*, pp. 380-88.

[14] Arden, *Augustana Heritage*, pp. 388-94.

[15] *Lutheran Companion*, 97, 16 July 1952, p. 9.

[16] Augustana Evangelical Lutheran Church, *Reports of the Ninety-Fourth Synod, June 9-14, 1953*, p. 340.

[17] "The Meaning of Lutheran Unity—A Proposed Blue Print," *Lutheran Companion*, 97, 5 November 1952. p. 10.

[18] *The One Holy Catholic Apostolic Church*, Rock Island: Augustana Book Concern, 1953, p. 91.

[19] "The Ecumenical Paradox— 'Our Oneness in Christ, Our Disunity as Churches,'" *Lutheran Companion*, 99, 4 August 1954, p. 8.

[20] The new name of the former Commission on Lutheran Unity, to which Bergendoff was elected in 1952.

[21] Minutes of the meeting of the Commission on Ecumenical Relations of the Augustana Lutheran Church, 15 November 1954, Minneapolis Minn, p. 4. Lutheran Church Collection, Archives, Gustavus Adolphus College, St. Peter, Minn.

[22] "What Kind of Lutheran Unity? Two Sign-Posts Point the Way," *Lutheran Companion*, 100, 19 January 1955, p. 11.

[23] "Augustana's Idea of the Church," *Augustana Seminary Review*, 7 (2), 1955, pp. 3-23.

[24] Published in Vilmos Vatja, ed, *The Unity of the Churches: A Symposium*, "Papers Presented to the Commissions on Theology and Liturgy of the Lutheran World Federation," Rock Island: Augustana Press, 1957, pp. 3-9.

[25] *The Doctrine of the Church in American Lutheranism*, Philadelphia: Board of Publications of the United Lutheran Church in America, 1956.

[26] Johannes Knudsen, *The Formation of the Lutheran Church in America*, Philadelphia: Fortress Press, 1978, p. 42.

[27] Minutes of the Joint Commission on Lutheran Unity, 12-13 December 1956, p. 13.

[28] W. Kent Gilbert, *Commitment to Unity: A History of the Lutheran Church in America*, Philadelphia: Fortress Press, 1988, pp. 105-07.

[29] Knudsen, *Formation*, p. 25.

[30] "Appendix G," Minutes of the Joint Commission on Lutheran Unity, 18 September 1957. See also p. 36.

[31] Knudsen, *Formation*, p. 62-63. From the context, I assume that Knudsen is suggesting that the discussions were hotly contested.

[32] "Conrad J.I. Bergendoff," in Robert Fischer, ed., *Franklin Clark Fry: A Palette for a Portrait*, n.p.: Supplementary Issue of the *Lutheran Quarterly*, 24, 1972, pp. 128-30. This volume is a series of remembrances of Fry, the ULCA President.

[33] Minutes of the Joint Commission on Lutheran Unity, 12 December 1957, pp. 54-57. See also Knudsen, *Formation*, pp. 61-65, and Gilbert, *Commitment to Unity*, p. 104.

[34] See "Appendix: Commission and Committee Memberships," Knudsen, *Formation*, pp.

121-26.

[35] Findings of the Conference on Lutheran Merger, Minneapolis Minn, 14-16 January 1959. Lutheran Church Collection, Dr. Leonard Kendall files, Archives, Gustavus Adolphus College, St. Peter, Minn.

[36] See Appendix D, Minutes of the Joint Lutheran Commission on Union, 5 March 1959. Though it is the fourth draft of the Constitution itself, the document notes that this is the *"first* highly provisional draft of the preamble." A fourth draft is found in the Minutes of 7 May 1959, and sixth draft in the Minutes of 6 July 1959.

[37] Knudsen, *Formation*, pp. 37-38.

[38] See Arden, *Augustana Heritage*, pp. 404-09.

[39] *Report of the Commission on Ecumenical Relations of the Augustana Evangelical Lutheran Church Concerning Merger Negotiations*, 1 June 1959.

[40] The address is printed in "Looking Ahead from 1960," *Lutheran Companion*, 105, 29 June 1960, pp. 3-4.

[41] On the formation of LCUSA, see Nelson, *Lutheranism in North America*, pp. 248-57, and Fendt, *The Struggle for Lutheran Unity*, pp. 264-299.

[42] *A Record of Doctrinal Conversations on Lutheran Cooperation Between the National Lutheran Council and the Lutheran Church-Missouri Synod, Lake Shore Club, Chicago, Illinois, July 7-9, 1960*, Records of 8 July 1960, in Fendt, *Struggle for Unity*, p. 271. Fendt has produced most of the records of these talks verbatim.

[43] "A Lutheran Study of Church Unity," *Essays on the Lutheran Confessions Basic to Lutheran Cooperation*, n.p., Published jointly by the Lutheran Church-Missouri Synod and the National Lutheran Council, 1961, p. 14.

[44] Fischer, ed., *Franklin Clark Fry*, p. 129.

[45] "Report of the Board of Theological Education," *Bulletin of Reports, Second Biennial Convention of the Lutheran Church in America*, Pittsburgh, Penn., 1964, p. 477.

[46] On this see Nelson, *Lutherans in North America*, pp. 219-20, and Gilbert, *Commitment to Unity*, pp. 162-3.

[47] Gilbert, p. 162.

111

NORTH STARS AND VASA ORDERS:
ON THE RELATIONSHIP BETWEEN SWEDEN
AND SWEDISH AMERICA

Dag Blanck

In 1938, Uppsala University conferred an honorary doctorate in theology on Conrad Bergendoff. At the time, Bergendoff had been president of Augustana College and Theological Seminary for three years and had established himself as a leading American scholar of the Swedish Reformation.[1] In addition, Bergendoff's theological ties with Sweden went back to the 1920s when he had worked together with Nathan Söderblom on ecumenical issues.

Conrad Bergendoff was not the first Swedish American to receive an honorary degree from a Swedish university. These academic institutions began recognizing Swedish-American scholarly and cultural achievements shortly before the turn of the century, when mass emigration had been underway for close to half a century. At Uppsala, for example. Olof Olsson and Carl A. Swensson, presidents of Augustana and Bethany colleges, received honorary degrees in 1893 and were followed by, among others, S. G. Öhman, a long-time pastor in New York in 1927, historians Amandus Johnson and George Stephenson in 1938, and Carl Sandburg in 1950.[2]

The awarding of honorary degrees can be seen as one part of a larger pattern of contacts between Sweden and Swedish America. There are many other indicators that can be used as well—literary and travel accounts being a particularly useful and fruitful source, as has recently been shown by H. Arnold Barton in his major study of the interrelationship between Sweden and Swedish America, *A Folk Divided*.[3] In this article I shall look at orders and medals awarded to Swedish Americans by the Swedish government as another example of how the "Old Country" interacted with and provided recognition of her emigrants and their children in the New World. I shall focus primarily on two medals, namely the Order of the North Star and the Vasa Order, both dating back to the eighteenth century. The North Star was awarded in recognition of scholarly and learned contribu-

112

tions as well as civic accomplishments. The Vasa Order recognized contributions to industry, trade, and agriculture as well as public service.

I

During the early phase of the emigration era, some homeland Swedes most frequently looked with skepticism at the burgeoning Swedish-American community on the other side of the Atlantic, portraying the emigrants, in H. Arnold Barton's words, "as vain seekers after purely material advantages, gullible dreamers, 'deserters,' and even violators of God's Sixth Commandment."[4] This was, as Barton also points out, a sentiment especially noticeable in conservative intellectual and religious circles in the country.[5] For example, the leadership of the Lutheran Augustana Synod, which had been founded by ministers ordained in the Church of Sweden and quickly became the leading denomination and largest organization in Swedish America, was concerned and alarmed that the Church of Sweden would favor the Episcopal Church in America and encourage Swedish immigrants to join that denomination instead of their Synod.[6]

By the turn of the century, however, it seems as if the relationship was improving. For example, in the early 1890s, when the faculty of Augustana Theological Seminary wrote to the Swedish bishops to ascertain how they viewed the Augustana Synod, six replied saying that they saw the Synod as the "daughter church" in America of the Church of Sweden.[7] Moreover, in 1893 on the occasion of the 300th anniversary of the Uppsala meeting of 1593, which marked the definitive implementation of the Swedish Reformation, the first Swedish bishop visited Swedish America in general and the Augustana Synod in particular, something that can be seen as a turning point in the relationship between at least the Augustana Synod and "official" Sweden.

An invitation had been extended by a group of Augustana ministers to the Church of Sweden to send a representative to the Swedish-American commemoration of this jubilee, and Knut Henning Gezelius von Schéele, professor of theology at Uppsala University from 1879 and bishop of Visby from 1885, was chosen to be the delegate.[8] Von Schéele took part in the major celebration in Rock Island in June 1893 as the official representative of the Church of

Sweden, and such leading figures in the Augustana Synod as Erik Norelius and P. J. Swärd welcomed him, noting with great pleasure that his visit marked the first recognition from the Church of Sweden that the Augustana Synod had received since its inception in 1860.[9] When the bishop was received in president Olsson's residence, it was noted that four or five hundred Swedish-American young people were in attendance to greet him, as "many of us Swedish Americans who have only seen the old country on a map" had "never seen such a bishop."[10]

Bishop Knut Henning Gezelius von Schéele.
(Courtesy of Augustana College Library, Special Collections.)

Von Schéele returned to America twice: in 1901 when he visited several of the Swedish-American colleges and was greeted as an old friend by the Augustana Synod, and in 1910 when the Augustana Synod and Augustana College celebrated their fiftieth anniversary on a grand scale in Rock Island. *Augustana*, the official organ of the Synod, commented that his visit in 1901 demonstrated that the Swedes in America were better appreciated in Sweden now than during the preceding five decades, attributing a major role to von Schéele for this shifting of attitudes.[11] Von Schéele, for his part, was obviously impressed by the intellectual and religious life he found during his visits to Swedish America. For example, in his account of his journey in 1893, he gives high praise to the Augustana Synod as the ecclesiastical body that has preserved the ancient Swedish faith in America,[12] and notes that the members of the graduating class at Augustana College in 1893 were of the same academic standard as would be found at comparable schools in Sweden.[13] He is especially impressed by the fact that many students in Gotland—his home province—would have a hard time measuring up to the level of expertise in Swedish language and literature demonstrated at Augustana College "by boys and girls born and raised in America."[14]

Von Schéele was thus one of the first representatives of the Swedish intellectual and religious establishment to visit the Augustana Synod and bring back positive impressions of it to Sweden. He also became an important contact for the Synod back in Sweden. For example, when Gustav Andreen, who would assume the presidency of Augustana College in 1901, prepared for a two-year study period spent at Uppsala University in 1898-1900, he was advised by Joshua Lindahl to "immediately call upon Bishop von Schéele," who could be of great assistance to Andreen in Uppsala.[15] Von Schéele did indeed assist Andreen in getting settled and establishing Swedish contacts. Moreover, Augustana pastors who returned to the Church of Sweden seem to have found a welcoming atmosphere in von Schéele's diocese in Visby.[16]

II

There seems to be a relationship between von Schéele's visits to America and the awarding of medals to Swedish Americans, especially to those connected with the Augustana Synod.[17] Although a few decorations had been awarded to Americans prior to 1893, they had all gone to Americans who had nothing to do with the Swedish-

American sphere, for example, several military officers, a U. S. diplomat in Sweden, and in 1863 the inventor and engineer John Ericsson.[18] The first medal bestowed on a Swedish American came after von Schéele's 1893 visit, when P. A. Swärd, president of the Augustana Synod, was made a commander, second class, of the North Star.

Between 1901 and 1910, eighteen orders were awarded to Swedish Americans, most of them affiliated with the Augustana Synod as pastors or professors at one of the Synod's colleges. Von Schéele's second visit in 1901 most likely provided the impetus for C. E. Lindberg, professor at Augustana Theological Seminary, C. A. Swensson, president of Bethany College, and Mattias Wahlström, president of Gustavus Adolphus College, all becoming commanders of the North Star that same year. In 1904, Gustav Andreen, from 1901 president of Augustana College, joined the ranks of these North Star commanders and was followed by Augustana Theological Seminary professor Nils Forsander in 1907. Ludvig Holmes, Augustana pastor in Burlington, Iowa—in the Augustana Synod "hailed as a kind of national poet"[19]—became a commander of the Vasa Order in 1908. He had already, however, received the medal *Litteris et Artibus*, given in recognition of his literary and artistic achievements in 1901, which had been bestowed on him by Bishop von Schéele during his second visit to America.[20]

In 1910, the Augustana Synod marked its fiftieth anniversary with a major ten-day celebration that June in Rock Island. This jubilee attracted a great number of people; and Swedish participants included not only Bishop von Schéele—now on his third trip to Swedish America—but also Henrik Schück, *rector magnificus* of Uppsala University. Greetings from various quarters in Swedish society including religious, governmental, and educational institutions, were conveyed, as well as from individuals such as the author Selma Lagerlöf and Uppsala University professor Adolf Noreen.[21]

If von Schéele's visit in 1893 marked the beginning of a new relationship between official Sweden and at least the Augustana sphere in Swedish America, the 1910 jubilee confirmed that the academic and state church community in Sweden now saw the Augustana Synod and its institutions as the established intellectual and spiritual center of Swedish America. Henrik Schück, for example, in his address at Rock Island described the role of Augustana College as "that place where Sweden and America join together, *Augustana Conciliatrix*, a patriotic institution of higher learning for the Swedish

Americans' both homelands: that large, new, and energetic country which has become theirs, and that old home where his forefathers rest, but over which the sun of memories will always shine."[22]

The 1910 jubilee also meant the bestowing of medals, and no less than ten were awarded to leading persons in the Augustana Synod that year. Some examples include North Star orders to Erik Norelius, Augustana Synod president, historian, founding father, and by 1910, patriarch of Swedish-American Lutheranism; L. G. Abrahamson, long-time editor of *Augustana*; and J. A. Udden, professor of geology at Augustana from 1888 and founder of the school's strong program in that field. In addition, Augustana College president Andreen received another medal, this time a Vasa Order, an honor he also shared with Augustana professor C. M. Esbjörn and long-time New York pastor Mauritz Stolpe, as well as with A. G. Anderson, the business manager of the Augustana Book Concern, the Synod's publishing house.

During the following decade another dozen active Swedish Americans received Swedish medals. Persons associated with the Augustana Synod were less dominant after 1910, and now the list also included journalists and writers such as Edwin Björkman, Charles Johansen, Alexander Johnson, Alexander Olsson, and Gustav N. Swan; the politician John Lind, the first of Swedish descent to become governor of Minnesota; and the businessmen N. A. Nelson and John Jeppson. This wider group of Swedish-American recipients of Swedish medals is certainly a sign of the broadening nature of contacts between Sweden and Swedish America, which meant that other groups besides the Augustana Synod began to be recognized in Sweden after 1910.

III

It is thus possible to notice a relationship between the timing of von Schéele's visits to Swedish America and the bestowing of medals on Swedish Americans. This connection is confirmed by an examination of recently discovered correspondence between the bishop and Augustana College president Gustav Andreen.

Obviously, certain persons in Sweden played important roles in promoting candidates for different orders, and von Schéele seems to have played a key role in promoting the interests of the Augustana Swedish Americans. One dimension of von Schéele's work in this regard, seems to have been to suggest Swedish-American candidates for Swedish decorations. In a January 1905 letter to Augustana College president Gustav Andreen, for example, von Schéele congratulates Andreen on having become a knight (*riddare*) of the North Star in 1904, adding that it was with "joy" that he had "played a role" in Andreen's nomination for the decoration.[23]

Sometimes, the candidates for Swedish decorations were discussed in considerable detail. For example, the suitability of Johan Enander, one of the best known Swedish Americans, long-time editor of *Hemlandet* and leading Swedish-American ideologue, was questioned by Bishop von Schéele in a letter to Gustav Andreen dated January 1905. Andreen seems to have suggested Enander's name to von Schéele, who, however, hesitated, saying that he was "unable [to] . . . support the proposed lesser decoration for Doctor Enander" at the present time. Still, the bishop asked Andreen how he felt about Enander's "old sins," as though a decoration for Enander might be possible it von Schéele were to visit America again in 1907.[24]

Andreen responded that he favored Enander's candidacy.[25] He noted that Enander's "great services" outweighed his "faults," the latter by now having been forgotten in Swedish America as well as greatly exaggerated in the first place. Andreen continued, assuring von Schéele that in the Swedish-American press none had done more for "the preservation of a genuine and patriotic Swedishness among us." Moreover, in 1903 a rumor to the effect that a decoration was forthcoming for Enander, had reached Swedish America; and the disappointment had been great when no medal was bestowed. Today, Andreen concludes, Enander is old, his "spirit broken," nor may he live long. "My sincere opinion is that if Dr. Enander were to be remembered, this would be greeted with the greatest satisfaction in all of Swedish America."

Andreen's advocacy must have convinced Bishop von Schéele to act on Enander's behalf, since a few months later (in May 1905) he could inform Andreen that he had been received at a private audience with the King and Crown Prince, where he requested "some kind of decoration for Enander."[26] It seemed impossible to make him a knight (*riddare*) of either the North Star or the Vasa Order "because of the way in which he left Sweden," but von Schéele was hopeful that he might be able to secure for Enander "the same decoration that [Ludvig] Holmes received," namely the *Litteris et Artibus* medal. Concurrently, von Schéele underscored that this information was confidential, as the King was "very restrictive with decorations."

Von Schéele's efforts on behalf of Enander were fruitful, and in

June 1905 the bishop could inform Andreen of his "success."[27] Enander's *Litteris et Artibus* medal would be presented in Chicago by pastor L. G. Abrahamson, who was "the oldest bearer of royal decorations in America [and was] suggested by me." The presentation was made at a banquet in the Windy City, which also marked the fiftieth anniversary of *Hemlandet*.[28]

Candidates for Swedish decorations also included individuals who had made or were thought to be able to make financial contributions to Swedish-American institutions; and these names were often suggested directly to von Schéele by leading Swedish Americans. One example is the Swedish-born lumber millionaire C. A. Smith from Minneapolis, who gave lumber worth $100,000 to Bethany College in Lindsborg, Kansas, in 1904[29] and who was made commander of the second class of the Vasa Order that same year.[30] Bishop von Schéele commented in a letter to Andreen that his "old friend" C. A. Swensson, the president of Bethany College "several times had asked me for a Vasa Order for him" and that he was happy he had been able to grant the request of a "deceased friend."[31] Another example is that of C. J. A. Ericsson of Boone, Iowa, a successful businessman and state senator,[32] who gave twelve acres of land valued at $25,000 to Augustana College in 1893[33] and made a further donation of $30,000 in 1901.[34] In 1905 Andreen suggested his name to Bishop von Schéele, as he had hopes that Ericsson would "remember our college with a still larger donation" and noting that Ericsson had the same relationship to Augustana as Smith had to Bethany.[35] Andreen's request on Ericsson's—and Augustana's—behalf, however, was unsuccessful.

It should also be noted that Gustav Andreen had become a knight of the North Star in 1904; and this was interpreted as one means of supporting a fundraising campaign on behalf of Augustana College since 1900 and one that sought to raise 100,000 Swedish crowns to pay for a professorship at the school. Early in 1903, Andreen visited Sweden to enlist further support for the campaign, and in 1904 it was announced that the well-known philanthropist Oscar Ekman in Gothenburg had donated half of the sum to the "Augustana fund," as it was called. Otto Elander, a Gothenburg newspaper editor and friend of Andreen, congratulated him for receiving the North Star in a 1905 letter and said that although he did not particularly care for "shiny medals," he thought they were useful when the "helped a *cause*" and added that "the North Star will be useful" for the fundraising drive "whose guardian" Andreen was.[36]

A later example of how a prominent Swede was enlisted in

support of the candidacy of a Swedish American for official Swedish recognition comes from 1938. In that year, Vilhelm Lundström, the head of *Riksföreningen för svenskhetens bevarande i utlandet* (the Society for the Preservation of Swedish Culture in Foreign Lands), made his one and only journey to the United States. In the 1920s Lundström had been disappointed with the efforts to preserve a sense of Swedishness in America and in particular, he had criticized the Augustana Synod for not maintaining the Swedish language.[37]

During his American trip, Lundström came to Augustana College—a visit that he, according to his diary, did not look forward to with "any great anticipation."[38] Nevertheless, he was pleasantly surprised with the school, its faculty and president, Conrad Bergendoff. He also noted that the president of the Synod, P. O. Bersell, did not seem as "anti-Swedish" as he had supposed him to be. When Augustana history professor O. Fritiof Ander suggested that a Swedish decoration of some kind might be suitable for Bersell, Lundström responded positively,[39] and although no further information is available, it does not seem unlikely that Lundström, who also was a highly respected professor of classics at the University of Gothenburg, may have played a role in the decision to confer an honorary degree from Uppsala University on Bersell in 1948.

IV

As H. Arnold Barton has emphasized, the relationship between Sweden and Swedish America, between the homeland and its children and grandchildren in the New World, was not always an easy one. It was strangely imbalanced—in some respects "a dialogue of the deaf;" and it often was characterized by misunderstandings.[40] The cultural and intellectual work in the Swedish-American community was a source of pride to Swedish Americans, who seem to have been especially sensitive to indifference or criticism from homeland Swedes regarding this dimension of their community's life.

In fact, Swedish Americans were eager for recognition of their cultural achievements from homeland Swedes. For example, Swedish-American publishers and authors often spent great energy on making certain that their works would be reviewed by Swedish critics and represented in Swedish libraries. Positive comments on Swedish-American culture by homeland Swedes also received great attention in Swedish America, and Birgitta Svensson has recently suggested

120

that an important dimension of the literary annual *Prärieblomman* (published by the Augustana Synod) was to present Swedish-American culture to the Old Country, or in her words, to be "a cultural manifestation directed at Sweden."[41]

Official recognition in the form of honorary degrees, medals, prizes, and awards became particularly important as status symbols for the Swedish Americans. When Ludvig Holmes had received his *Litteris et Artibus* in 1901, this event was featured prominently even in the local English-language press in Holmes' hometown of Burlington, Iowa.[42] Honorary degrees were awarded to Swedish Americans by both their own colleges and by Swedish universities. As the number of degrees conferred by Swedish universities were fewer, these seem to have been the more coveted ones.

The list of Swedish medals awarded to people living in the United States shows that it was not until the 1890s that organized Swedish America was so recognized by official Sweden. It is also clear that Bishop K. H. G. von Schéele played an important role in promoting Swedish-American candidates. The years around the turn of the century mark a turning point in the relationship between Sweden and Swedish America, when elements of the Swedish establishment began to recognize and respect their countrymen's intellectual and cultural achievements on the other side of the Atlantic.

The list of recipients shows, moreover, that once this turning point had been reached, it was persons associated with the Augustana Synod who most frequently were honored, suggesting that it was the Augustana sphere in Swedish America that became most closely linked with official Sweden. It is telling that up until 1931 few representatives of other Swedish-American denominations received any medals—one notable exception being David Nyvall, who became a knight of the Vasa Order in 1929. This was especially true up until about 1915, when the scope broadened markedly, something that may have been related to the fact that the Augustana Synod was changing and becoming more "American." This was perhaps most vividly reflected in the transition from the Swedish to the English language in the Synod, which had begun already in 1908 with the establishment of the Association of English Churches, but which accelerated rapidly in the 1920s.[43] Especially the loss of the language, which was such an emotional issue, may have made official Sweden pay greater attention to other groups that were promoting the usage of Swedish more actively than was the Augustana Synod.

Finally, it is interesting to note that at least on two occasions, two different Swedish-American college presidents sought to use the recognition that a Swedish medal gave by suggesting names of candidates to Bishop von Schéele, hoping that this honor might make the candidate more willing to support their respective institutions. In at least one case, this strategy proved successful.

It took official Sweden a little less than half a century to recognize much of the cultural and intellectual work that was going on in Swedish America. The initial indifference or even disdain shown by the Old Country was replaced by a new interest in the developments in Swedish America, at times in highly laudatory terms.[44] The fact that Swedish medals began to be bestowed on leading Swedish Americans is a good indication of the degree of acceptance that Swedish America had achieved in official Swedish circles, as, in the eyes of official Sweden, the poor Swedish emigrant farmers, crofters, and laborers had now become Swedish-American ministers, professors, and professionals—worthy of both North Star and Vasa orders.

NOTES

[1] His *Olavus Petri and the Swedish Reformation* was published by Macmillan Press in 1928. Down to the present day, this work remains a standard English-language treatment of the subject.

[2] Torgny Nevéus, ed., *Honoris Causa. Hedersdoktorer och hedersmedlemmar. Uppsala universitet 1839-1992* (Uppsala, 1992). I wish to thank Harald Runblom for supplying me with this information.

[3] H. Arnold Barton, *A Folk Divided: Homeland Swedes and Swedish Americans, 1840-1940* (Carbondale, Ill., 1994).

[4] H. Arnold Barton, "Swedish Reactions to the Emigration Question Around the Turn of the Century," *Swedish-American Historical Quarterly*, 44 (1993): 90.

[5] Barton, "Swedish Reactions," 89-90.

[6] See George Stephenson, *The Religious Aspects of Swedish Immigration* (Minneapolis, 1932), 214-18 and Bernhard Erling, "Augustana, Bishops, and the Church of Sweden," *Lutheran Forum*, 26 (1992): 46-48.

[7] *Augustana*, 14 April 1892.

[8] H. Arnold Barton, *A Folk Divided*, 96-97.

[9] *Augustana*, 14 and 22 June 1893.

[10] *Augustana*, 8 June 1893.

[11] *Augustana*, 5 December 1901.

[12] K. H. G. von Schéele, *Hemlandstoner. En hälsning från modern Svea till dotterkyrkan i Amerika* (Stockholm, 1894), 3-6.

[13] von Schéele, *Hemlandstoner*, 151.

[14] von Schéele, *Hemlandstoner*, 152. Cf. also von Schéele's extremely positive speech at the celebrations in Rock Island (*Augustana*, 22 June 1893).

[15] Joshua Lindahl to Gustav Andreen, Cincinnati, Ohio, 6 July 1898. In the Andreen Papers, Special Collections, Augustana College Library, Rock Island, Illinois.

[16] Sten Carlsson, "Augustana Lutheran Pastors in the Church of Sweden," *Swedish-American Historical Quarterly*, 35 (1984), 241-42.

[17] All of the subsequent information about numbers of medals and orders, as well as individual recipients, is based on a compliation made by Vilhelm Berger, *Svenska ordnar och medaljer i Förenta Staterna* (New York, 1931). According to the preface, Berger has based his list on an examination of *Sveriges statskalender* between 1884 and 1931, as well as notices of awards in the Swedish-American press. For this article I have extracted those individuals who in some way were part of organized Swedish America.

[18] Some examples include: *Svärdsorden*: Col. T. P. Shaffner, 1864; *Vasaorden*: cols. Thom Scott and Meyer Ash and Gen. A. Francis Walker, 1877, Richard Somers Smith, U.S. Consul in Stockholm, 1880; *Nordstjärneorden*: Edward Williams, 1877.

[19] Eric Johannesson, "Scholars, Pastors and Journalists: The Literary Canon of Swedish-America," in Dag Blanck & Harald Runblom, eds., *Swedish Life in American Cities* (Uppsala, 1991), 96.

[20] Johannesson, "Scholars, Pastors and Journalists," 99.

[21] For an account of the jubilee, see *Minnen från jubelfesten. Program, predikningar och tal vid Augustana College och Augustana-synodens femtioårsjubileum den 5-15 juni 1910* (Rock Island, Ill., 1911).

[22] *Minnen från jubelfesten*, 115.

[23] K. H. G. von Schéele to Gustav Andreen, Stockholm, 24 January 1905. In the Gustav Andreen Papers (uncatalogued addition), Special Collections, Augustana College Library (GAPuncat).

[24] *Ibid.*

[25] The following is based on an undated draft [February 1905?] of a letter from Gustav Andreen in Rock Island to K. H. G. von Schéele, GAPuncat.

[26] The following is based on K. H. G. von Schéele to Gustav Andreen, Stockholm, 18 May 1905, GAPuncat.

[27] The following is based on K. H. G. von Schéele to Gustav Andreen, Stockholm, 7 June 1905, GAPuncat.

[28] Cf. Johan Enander, "En svensk-amerikansk tidnings 50 års-jubileum," *Prärieblomman. Kalender för 1906* (Rock Island, Ill., 1905), 241.

[29] Emory Lindquist, *Smoky Valley People: A History of Lindsborg, Kansas* (Lindsborg, Kan., 1953), 237. In the early 1890s, Smith also gave money to the short-lived Emanuel Academy in Minneapolis and in 1902, to Gustavus Adolphus College to promote a move of that school from St. Peter to St. Paul, Minnesota. See Stephenson, *Religious Aspects of Swedish Immigration*, 344, 361.

[30] *Sveriges statskalender för 1907* (Uppsala, 1907), 576.

[31] K. H. G. von Schéele to Gustav Andreen, Stockholm, 24 January 1905, GAPuncat.

[32] Adolph Benson and Naboth Hedin, eds., *Swedes in America 1638-1938* (New Haven, 1938), 325.

[33] Benson and Hedin, *Swedes in America*, 160.

[34] *Referat öfver förhandlingarna vid Augustana-Synodens fyrtioandra årsmöte i Jamestown, N.Y. 1901* (Rock Island, Ill., 1901), 21.

[35] Gustav Andreen to K. H. G. von Schéele, Rock Island, undated draft [February 1905?], GAPuncat.

[36] Otto Elander to Gustav Andreen, Gothenburg, 12 January 1905, GAPuncat.

[37] Cf. H. Arnold Barton's article in this issue.

[38] Bengt Bogärde, *Vilhelm Lundström och svenskheten* (Gothenburg, 1992), 86.

[39] *Ibid.*

[40] Barton, *A Folk Divided*, 396.

[41] Birgitta Svensson, *Den omplanterade svenskheten. Kulturell självhävdelse och etnisk medvetenhet i den svensk-amerikanska kalendern Prärieblomman 1900-1913* (Gothenburg, 1994), ch. 5.

[42] Johannesson, "Scholars, Pastors and Journalists," 99.

[43] Sture Lindmark, *Swedish America, 1914-1932. Studies in Ethnicity with Emphasis on Illinois and Minnesota* (Stockholm and Chicago, 1971), 261-66, 276-83.

[44] See, for example, the writings of Carl Sundbeck: *Svensk-amerikanerna. Deras materiella och andliga sträfvanden* (Rock Island, Ill., 1902) and *Svensk-Amerika lefve! Några tal hållna i Amerika* (Stockholm, 1904).

THE FOURTH R—RELIGIOUS EDUCATION IN SWEDEN AND THE USA

BERNHARD ERLING

This comparison between Sweden and the USA concentrates attention especially on the religious education provided in the public sector for the children of all the citizens. Conrad Bergendoff, to whom this essay is dedicated, has devoted his life to church related higher education, first as dean of Augustana Theological Seminary, then president of Augustana College and Theological Seminary, and, after the two institutions were separated, president of Augustana College. Most Lutheran church related higher education has presupposed the education offered in the public schools. Though the Augustana Synod did for a time maintain some schools offering secondary education, the public schools were accepted for elementary education and also for secondary education, when this became generally available.[1] It was thought that the Church and the home could provide the religious education that in the USA was not being offered in the public schools. There is reason to question whether this way of providing for religious education is any longer wholly adequate. Despite the great value of what can be accomplished in the home and the local congregation, not all parents do provide sufficient religious teaching in the home, and it is extremely difficult to find sufficient time to teach all that should be taught in church sponsored religious education classes. Furthermore, too many American children are not enrolled in these classes, while many who are, fail to attend them regularly. The same is true in varying degrees for other religious groups in the American society. Some would ask, therefore, whether an effort should not be made to incorporate to a much greater extent religious education also in the public school curriculum.

For both Sweden and the USA including religious education in the curriculum of the public schools has posed a problem due to the fact of religious pluralism. These two countries have responded to this problem in different ways. The USA has sought to remove religious content as much as possible from public education, whereas Sweden has, especially in recent years, developed a curriculum that takes into

125

account this pluralism, instructs pupils about it, and also helps them define what their own faith orientation is to be. In what follows, the account of religious education in Sweden will be given first, thereafter what has happened with respect to this aspect of the curriculum in the USA. There will then be some concluding observations.

I

During the past four hundred years, three phases concerning religious education in Sweden can be distinguished: first, a period marked by strong efforts to achieve and maintain religious unity; second, a period during which the insistence on religious unity was gradually and slowly relaxed; and third, a time in recent decades when an attempt has been and is being made to adapt the curriculum of the Swedish public schools to the implications of acceptance of religious pluralism for religious education.

Religious Unity in Sweden

While the sixteenth-century Lutheran Reformation in Sweden called for significant changes in religious teaching and practice, it also represented an effort to achieve religious unity. In 1527 it was decreed that everywhere in the kingdom God's word should be preached in its purity. By 1541 a group led by Olavus Petri (who, with his brother, Laurentius Petri, had studied in Wittenberg) completed the translation of the Bible into Swedish. In 1544 a hymnal that also contained Luther's Small Catechism was published. In 1571 Laurentius Petri, then archbishop of Uppsala, wrote an evangelical church order (which also included Sweden's first school order), establishing a norm for liturgical practice and polity. Though there was no specific reference to confessions, preaching the gospel was defined as preaching forgiveness of sins in the name of Jesus Christ, and in relation thereto preaching repentance.

Problems arose as after Laurentius Petri's death in 1573 King Johan III introduced a controversial liturgy, bringing back certain Roman Catholic practices. There were, furthermore, fears when the king died in 1592 that his son, Sigismund, who had been strongly influenced by his Polish Roman Catholic mother and who was already king of Roman Catholic Poland, might try to promote the

126

Counter-Reformation in Sweden. Those who wanted Sigismund to be required at his coronation to promise to rule in accord with an evangelical confession organized the Uppsala Assembly, which met from 1-20 March 1593. It was proposed that Sweden adopt the Augsburg Confession, which was read and discussed article by article. When it was finally adopted the chairman of the assembly exclaimed, "Now has Sweden become one man, and we all have one Lord and God!"[2]

At his coronation Sigismund promised to rule in accord with the Augsburg Confession. He continued to reside in Poland, delegating authority in Sweden to a regent, his uncle, Duke Karl. Disagreement between the two developed and in 1598 King Sigismund attacked Duke Karl's forces and was defeated at the battle of Stångebro. As a result the following year Sigismund lost the crown of Sweden and Karl ruled in his place, though he did not agree to coronation until 1607. King Karl IX was succeeded at his death in 1611 by his son, Gustaf II Adolf. A series of laws and decrees in 1604 (*Norrköpings arvförening*), 1617 (*Örebro stadga*), and 1634 (*1634 års regeringsreform*), stipulated that the kingdom required unity in religion and that any crown prince who fell away from God's pure word and the unaltered Augsburg Confession would thereby have lost his claim to the throne.[3] Later theological controversies between advocates of different interpretations of Lutheran orthodoxy led to a decree in 1663 that departure from pure doctrine, by which was meant the teachings set forth in the Augsburg Confession and interpreted in the other Lutheran confessional writings in the Book of Concord, could be punishable by death. This point of view was later reaffirmed in the Church Law of 1686, which stated that everyone in Sweden, as well as in lands subject to its crown, should confess the pure evangelical doctrine as defined in the Lutheran confessions. Those failing to confess this faith should be exiled. In the Church Law of 1686, which though revised in various ways was to remain in force for 300 years, it was presupposed that Swedish society was a unity and that the Church of Sweden included the whole population. The church was accordingly firmly in control of education. While there was not yet obligatory education for all the citizens, it was deemed desirable that people should be enabled to understand the doctrine taught in the church. Pastors were required to preach catechetical sermons and to know the members of their parishes well enough so that they could indicate in the church books the degree of each person's understanding of Christianity.[4]

The first threat to this religious unity in Sweden came during the early eighteenth century from pietism. The word's original meaning was negative and referred to what was regarded as excessive, exaggerated piety, more especially individualistic forms of piety that emerged in opposition to the collective church life of orthodoxy. Pietistic movements developed throughout Europe and the pietism that came to Sweden had its origins in Germany. Students who had studied at German universities, especially at the University of Halle, a center of German pietism, came home as its zealous promoters. Soldiers who fought for Charles XII and became prisoners of war read pietist devotional writings during their imprisonment. After release from prison they came home bringing with them this literature.[5] What troubled the authorities was that the pietists met in small groups and it was impossible to tell whether the ideas they shared were theologically acceptable.

In 1726 the Swedish government issued the Conventicle Decree. It was based on the statement in the Church Law of 1686 that strictly forbade "conceiving and spreading any misleading ideas." The decree forbade persons, whether members of the local parish or of other parishes, few or many, to meet in homes in the absence of a pastor under the pretext of having devotions, or, more specifically, to hold a service. The intent was to preserve unity in religion. To contribute to this end pastors were instructed to hold cottage meetings to examine the faith of the people, which led to the development of what were known as *husförhör* (catechetical meetings held in homes throughout a parish). A negative consequence of the Conventicle Decree was that lay people were kept from participating in church activities, which drove Swedish pietism in more radical directions.

Religious Unity Requirement Gradually Relaxed

The Conventicle Decree did make an exception for foreigners of the Anglican and Reformed faiths, and in 1741 these denominations received permission to build churches in port cities. This tolerance was widened in 1781-82 to include the whole kingdom and all Christian foreigners, as well as Jews. Despite efforts to gain even greater religious freedom and some movement in this direction in the Constitution of 1809, it was not until 1858 that the Conventicle Decree was repealed.

During the nineteenth century there was further relaxation of the rigor of the legislation designed to insure religious unity in Sweden. In 1860 the law stipulating punishment for those who departed from the pure evangelical doctrine was repealed and the possibility to withdraw from the Church of Sweden was granted. Permission was also given to form one's own Christian congregation, if the king gave his consent. The person who wanted to withdraw was, however, to be taught, exhorted, and warned both by the pastor of his congregation and the cathedral chapter. In 1873 the requirements for withdrawing from the Church of Sweden were modified so that a waiting period of two months replaced the requirement of being taught, exhorted, and warned about what withdrawal would mean. In 1892 the only condition for the right to withdraw was that one had to indicate the Christian communion one was entering, though this communion did not need to be one already recognized by the state.

During the nineteenth century a number of free churches, whose doctrine, administration, and economy were not dependent on the state, were organized, some as a result of Anglo-American influences. The first Baptist congregation was organized in 1848 and in 1873 the first Methodist Episcopal congregation was organized. In 1878 the Swedish Mission Covenant was organized, a free church that grew out of the Evangelical National Foundation, a movement for renewal within the Church of Sweden. In part the stimulus that led to the formation of this denomination was a doctrinal controversy over Paul Peter Waldenström's interpretation of the doctrine of the atonement. He insisted that the New Testament did not teach that Jesus' death was necessary in order to turn aside God's wrath directed against the sinner. Waldenström taught that a loving God was always ready freely to forgive the sinner. At this point he took issue with the Lutheran confessions and as a result the Mission Covenant in its constitution did not adopt any confessions, basing its teaching simply on the Holy Scriptures.[6]

Religious Education and Religious Pluralism

General public education began in Sweden in 1842 with the introduction of the obligatory folk school. The church strongly supported public education so that the laity might be enabled to read the Bible and the catechism. These schools provided the setting for the church's catechetical instruction, the teaching of evangelical Lutheran doctrine, with its goal of forming persons into Christian members of society. The diocesan cathedral chapters were responsible for the preparation of teachers, while in the parishes the education provided was given under the supervision of the senior pastor. It was not until 1930 that the supervision of these schools became a communal rather than a churchly affair.[7]

The first adaptation of the religious education curriculum to the religious pluralism that had developed in Sweden, occurred in 1919 when it was decided to remove Luther's Small Catechism from the folk school religious education curriculum.[8] By this time it was recognized that various groups, such as the labor movement, the temperance movement, and the free churches all had a legitimate interest in the schools. The non-confessional stance of the Mission Covenant and the Baptists contributed to the decision. While the school was to remain Christian, it was to have a more general religious orientation. In the place of the Catechism greater stress was to be placed on biblical texts, especially those imparting moral teaching that would be acceptable to all. Much attention was given to the Sermon on the Mount. The aim of this education was to promote moral development.

In the decades that followed, two important problems were considered: the question of religious freedom and the question of how to develop a curriculum that could be common for all. Two important reports dealt with these questions, the 1940 *skolutredning* (school investigation) and the 1946 *skolkommission* (school commission). The 1940 report took note of the 1919 curricular plan and stressed Christianity as a communal factor that could contribute to the nurture of citizens. Pupils were therefore not only to be taught empirically verifiable facts but should be given an experience of how important the religious and historical fellowship is. The 1946 report, on the other hand, stressed the ideals of democratization and secularization. It regarded religion as a private affair. Ethical nurture should not be related to a particular religious-ethical ideal, but to a more general humanistic one. No single ethical alternative should be preferred, but several options should be presented with the decision being made by the individual, concerning both personal and social issues. At the same time it was presupposed that the instruction would indicate the community's need for such ethical norms as honesty, helpfulness, and the willingness to cooperate.[9]

The next important date concerning religious education in Sweden is the 1951 law granting the right of unconditional withdrawal from the Church of Sweden. The Swedish Parliament (*riksdag*) had expressed itself in favor of such a law in 1909 and the bishops and the church assembly had given their support to this idea in 1929, but not until 1951 was this law enacted. The right to teach Christianity in the public schools was given to members of a specified list of Swedish denominations, as well as to those who in writing stated that they did not hold views in conflict with the teachings of evangelical Christianity. There was discussion of whether one could teach independently of one's own convictional orientation and there began to be reference to objective religious education. Further implications of the 1951 religious freedom law were drawn in 1962 when the nine-year Comprehensive School (*grundskolan*) was established and received its first curricular plan. According to this plan the school became non-confessional and the Church of Sweden no longer had any formal influence on the school. Pupils were to be given information *about* Christianity *and* other religions. The plan stated that the instruction was to be objective.

With regard to the development from 1919 to 1962, in the former year Christianity was accepted as providing the primary motivation for the communal ethic. One sought to interpret Christianity in such a way that it could be accepted by as many as possible. In 1962 (even though statistically for most of the population Christianity was still the basis for the communal ethic) as secularization had progressed, the fact that many were choosing to base the communal ethic on other convictional orientations was also recognized. It was assumed, however, that all could agree about certain fundamental democratic values. The Curricular Plan (*läroplan för grundskolan*, 1962) stated:

> Through its ethical nurture the school shall give the pupil a good understanding of the moral norms which must apply as people live together and which undergird the order of law in a democratic community. He must become fully conscious of the meaning of ethical concepts such as justice, honesty, consideration and tolerance, and of the consequences of infractions against laws and precepts. . . . The main task of the social nurture, which the school's teaching is also to include, is to awaken respect for truth and justice, for human dignity, for inviolability of human life and thereby for the right to personal integrity.[10]

In 1969 the Comprehensive School received its second Curricular Plan (*lgr* 69). What had been called "teaching about Christianity" now

131

was renamed "teaching about religion." The requirement that the instruction be objective remained. It was to be factual and comprehensive and give such knowledge that the pupil be able to choose from among different life orientations. The school itself was to be neutral.

In the Curricular Plan of 1980 there was a new development in that religious education was to concentrate on the pupils' life questions, as well as matters having to do with the environment. Pupils were to receive "a widened understanding of the Christian religion with the Bible in the center," but at the same time they should be enabled to compare the Christian heritage with other religious traditions, so that they could see how basic vital questions are answered in the context of different life orientations. That there are valuable contributions in the religious traditions many immigrants have brought to Sweden was to be acknowledged. The values of other cultures were to be respected, though anything that strives against the basic values of Swedish democracy was to be resisted.[11] Sweden has responded to the fact that immigrants have brought with them many different religious traditions. In the last three grades (7-9) of the Comprehensive School, religion has been included in the field of social studies, which also include social science, history, religion, and geography. In a two-volume textbook combining these different subjects, written for the seventh and eighth grades by Arne Lindquist and Jan Wester, besides Christianity the following religions are studied: Judaism, Islam, Hinduism, Buddhism, religions of China and Japan, and primitive religions.[12] Sven-Åke Selander points out that in the curricular plans from 1962 to 1980 there was a development from a closed to an open curriculum, from concentrating on Christianity to concentrating on community. Whereas earlier one had sought scientifically to describe and objectively to present Christianity, one now sought to describe and present religion and life orientation. In the place of terms such as "God," one now used more open ones such as "life."[13]

The most recent development is to be found the Curricular Plan of 1994.[14] Its name has been changed from the "Curricular Plan for the Comprehensive School and the Gymnasium" to the "Curricular Plan for the Obligatory School System and the Voluntary School Forms." The plan opens with this statement of basic values:

The public school system rests on the basis of democracy. . . The school has an important task to transmit and make secure

132

in the pupils the values that our social life rests upon. The inviolability of human life, the freedom and integrity of the individual, the equal value of all persons, the equality of women and men, as well as solidarity with the weak and the vulnerable, are the values that the school shall form and transmit. In accordance with the ethic prescribed by Christian tradition and Western humanism this happens through the individual's nurture toward a sense of justice, generosity, tolerance, and taking responsibility. The instruction in the school shall be non-confessional. The task of the school is to let each pupil find her/his unique identity and thereby be able to participate in the life of the community through giving her/his best in responsible freedom.[15]

Swedish curricular plans contain course descriptions. Somewhat new in 1994 as far as religion is concerned, is that both the content of religious knowledge and its existential aspect are to be held together. Pupils are to be given the possibility to use their own reflections and questions in working with existential and ethical problems so as to be able to arrive at a position of their own. They are to be made acquainted with the Christian tradition but also with such alternatives to the traditional religions as agnostic and atheistic life orientations.[16] Selander states that there has been development in the understanding of objectivity from the interpretation in the 1960s, that one could not influence the pupils, to the view that one may now help them with their problems as they think about what life orientation they have or would want to have. One does not prescribe what the choice should be; objectivity consists in helping pupils with problems that arise as they think about these matters. At the same time one provides factual and comprehensive information about the alternatives that might be considered. Selander also states that in this new curricular plan the religion requirement at the gymnasium level (grades 10-12), where there are a number of programs among which pupils may choose, has been increased so that those attending schools offering vocational instruction will also study religion. These students were formerly not required to study this subject during their last three years. The older conception that a Swedish understanding of democracy was sufficient as a basis for ethical behavior has, furthermore, been questioned. It is now being recognized that the religious as well as non-religious foundations on which the idea of Swedish democracy rests should be studied by all the pupils, whichever of the options they choose for the last three years of the one-to-twelve-year educational system.[17]

Quite clearly Sweden has come a long way in the 400 years since the Uppsala Assembly of 1593, when significant religious unity was achieved. During the last two centuries pluralism in faith and life orientations has developed in this Nordic country. Along with the Church of Sweden there are several free churches. Marxism, humanism, and atheism have been proposed as viable life orientations and recent immigration has brought religions such as Islam, Hinduism, and Buddhism to Sweden. Nonetheless the nation continues to require the inclusion of religious education throughout its twelve-year public educational system.

II

When Sweden and the United States are compared, it must at the outset be stated that there is no event in American history like the Uppsala Assembly of 1593, when for Sweden the Lutheran interpretation of Christianity became established. Instead, the USA has come to adopt the principle that religion should as much as possible be separated from the governmental process and consequently also from education that is publicly supported. This latter implication of the nonestablishment principle was not at first fully recognized. In order to understand how the principle of nonestablishment came to imply the exclusion of the study of religion from public education, we must examine the history of education in the USA.

The story begins with the colonial period. Prior to the American Revolution, there were three main divisions in the European settlement on the east coast of North America: the New England, the Middle, and the Southern colonies. The New England colonies were settled by dissenters from the Church of England, who thought of themselves as a new Israel with a divine commission to establish a godly commonwealth in the American wilderness. Early on they established schools. Boston Latin School dates back to 1635 and Harvard University, the oldest one in North America, was founded in 1636. The spirit of the Puritan founders of Harvard is expressed in these words:

> After God had carried us safe to New England, and wee had builded our houses, provided necessaries for our livelihood, rear'd convenient places for God's worship and settled the Civill Government; One of the next things we longed for, and

134

looked after, was to advance Learning and perpetuate it to Posterity; dreading to leave an illiterate Ministry to the churches, when our present ministers shall lie in the dust.[18]

In the Middle colonies there was much less homogeneity in the population. In New York and Delaware there were remnants of Dutch and Swedish colonies that had been taken over by the British. In Pennsylvania many Germans had settled. While all of these groups were Protestant, in Maryland there were Roman Catholics. The absence of a common language and the lack of religious uniformity made it difficult to establish common schools, as in New England. The elementary education that was to be found, was provided in private schools or by the different religious groups in each community. It took much longer in the Middle colonies to establish institutions of higher education. The oldest university in this section of the country is Princeton, founded in 1746, more than a century after the founding of Harvard.

In the Southern colonies the dominant church during the colonial period was the established Church of England. Here the College of William and Mary was founded in Williamsburg, Virginia, in 1693. There were, however, three problems that the Southern colonies faced. The nature of the first settlements was quite different from those in New England. Those who sponsored these settlements were primarily interested in financial profits that were to be returned to England. The earliest immigrants in Virginia have been described as "alumni of the Elizabethan and Jacobean culture of poverty, who had no intention of working, who squabbled with each other and fought with the Indians, and who died of mysterious diseases."[19] When later a plantation economy based on tobacco and slavery developed, families lived on large land holdings and were scattered over large areas, so that it was difficult to form either congregations or schools for the children. Finally, during and after the Revolutionary War, the identification of the Church of England with the British government, against which the colonists had revolted, weakened its influence in these colonies. The Church had, however, not given much attention to education and the State did not consider education its responsibility, either. There were tutors in homes, some small private schools, and a few pauper schools for children of the poorer classes.[20]

These differences between the colonies help explain why the dominant influence in the formation of early American culture during the colonial period and for some time thereafter came from Puritan

135

New England. In much of New England the Congregational churches were established, in the sense that they were publicly supported and linked with the government of each local community. In Massachusetts they so remained until 1833. Though the Church of England was established in some of the other colonies, as far as the nation itself was concerned, it was evident that the model of a federal ecclesiastical establishment would not be acceptable. Immediately upon the adoption of the federal Constitution, Congress proposed ten amendments, known as the Bill of Rights. The first of these begins: "Congress shall make no law respecting an establishment of religion, or prohibiting the free exercise thereof."[21] It is through this amendment, adopted in 1791, that separation of church and state has come to characterize American society.

Two things should be noted about this section of the First Amendment. First, when it was adopted it applied only to the federal government. In 1791 only Virginia and Rhode Island had full disestablishment,[22] though there was a growing number of Americans who belonged to religious groups, such as the Baptists, who in Europe had experienced suppression from established churches and who were opposed in principle to granting one religious group the privilege and power that establishment would provide. Thus, while this amendment did not make such a church-state relationship illegal on the state level, it was perhaps inevitable that the nonestablishment principle, due to increasing religious pluralism, would eventually be extended to the states. As new states adopted constitutions, many of them borrowed this language from the federal Constitution. The second thing to be noted is that no thought had been given to the implications of the nonestablishment principle as far as education was concerned. There is no reference to education in either the federal Constitution or the Federalist Papers. In the Middle and Southern states education was provided, for the most part, either in private or parish schools; it is possible that no extensive involvement of even local government in the educational process was anticipated. In New England, where there were publicly supported common schools, it was understood that the First Amendment applied only to the federal government, which had not yet begun to concern itself with education.[23]

New England, despite the strict Calvinism of its established Congregational churches, was not immune to the religious pluralism that was beginning to make itself felt throughout all the states. The Puritan requirement of experienced conversion for full church membership had been changed so that there could be a "half-way covenant" for those who were baptized but had not been converted. This half-way covenant did not admit them to holy communion but did permit them to have their children baptized. In the middle of the 18th century a revival, the Great Awakening, swept through the colonies dividing old denominations and creating new ones. Some theologians, who reacted negatively to certain aspects of the revival, took a more optimistic view of human nature than was taught by the orthodox Calvinists. They also stressed the humanity of Jesus and began to question the doctrine of the Trinity. This kind of thinking eventually led to division in the Congregational churches in eastern Massachusetts so that most of them became Unitarian. All of this obviously resulted in considerable doctrinal controversy.[24]

Some of the defenders of orthodoxy were unwise in their strict interpretation of Calvinism. One of them, Nathanael Emmons, was minister in Franklin, Massachusetts, for fifty-four years. In his rural parish lived the family of Horace Mann, who was to be the first secretary of the Massachusetts Board of Education. In 1810, when Horace was 14 years old, his older brother, Stephen, drowned on a Sunday, having failed to attend the service that day. At his funeral Nathanael Emmons spoke of the terrible last judgment and the lake that burns with fire and brimstone and left no doubt as to Stephen's eternal fate. Horace reacted strongly against such teaching and later became a Unitarian.[25] In 1827, probably in reaction to the doctrinal controversies that attended the emergence of the Unitarian denomination in 1825, the Massachusetts legislature enacted a law stating that the Committee on Education "shall never direct any school books to be purchased or used, in any schools under their superintendence, which are calculated to favor any particular religious sect or tenet."[26] Horace Mann became secretary of the Board of Education in 1837. He was in full agreement with the 1827 law and proposed that in the place of sectarian doctrines, ethics and only what can be known about God through a study of nature be taught in the common schools. With respect to Christianity, he argued that, since its teachings must be found in the Bible, reading the Bible without comment or interpretation should be sufficient.[27]

Horace Mann's way of solving the problem of defining the religious element in public education set the pattern for public schools in other parts of the nation. Not everyone was satisfied. Some thought that what Mann said should be taught about religion, sounded too Unitarian. Those least satisfied were Roman Catholics, who through immigration were becoming increasingly numerous. They regarded the common Christianity being taught in the public schools as a watered-down Protestantism. The King James Version of the Bible that was being read was to them a Protestant Bible. As to reading it without comment, Roman Catholics insisted that to understand the Bible one needed the guidance of the church.[28]

Roman Catholics proposed that instead of common schools there should be tax support for confessional schools, chosen according to parental preference. This proposal the Protestants opposed, since they felt that common schools were essential to achieve national unity. In order, however, to make the public schools as acceptable as possible to the Roman Catholics, Protestants agreed to the removal of more and more explicit religious content from the curriculum. This did not satisfy the Roman Catholics; where they could, especially in urban areas, they established their own schools. A few other denominations, among them some Lutherans, have done the same. Most Protestants, however, have supported the public school, since they have felt that the home and the local congregation could adequately supplement the education received in the public school.

In the development thus far surveyed, it should be emphasized that there was no intentional exclusion of religious teaching as such from the public schools. It was taken for granted that religion belonged in public education, but those in charge of the public schools simply could not cope with the problem of religious pluralism. Almost all specific religious teaching appeared to be sectarian and thus it was feared that teaching it under state auspices would violate someone's rights of conscience.

While the nonestablishment of religion provision in the federal Constitution was, as indicated above, often written into state constitutions, it was through the 14th Amendment adopted in 1868 that this principle was made applicable in all the states. The 14th Amendment had as its purpose to make certain that individual southern states would not deprive the recently freed slaves of the rights that should, following their emancipation, be theirs as free United States citizens. While this amendment did not effectively safeguard the rights of black citizens, it has in this century provided the basis for important civil rights decisions. The United States Supreme Court interpreted the 14th Amendment to mean that all the rights and freedoms provided in the other amendments, which had originally referred only to the federal government, could now be claimed in all the other governmental jurisdictions. Thus the federal nonestablishment principle became applicable not only to all the states, whether their constitutions contained such a provision or not, but also to each local school board.

Within the last fifty years this implication of the 14th Amendment has led to a series of changes as far as religion in the public schools is concerned. Suits have been filed by parents who have claimed that the rights of their children have been violated by released time religious education classes held on school premises,[29] by the recitation of a prayer prescribed by the state board of education,[30] or by the reading without comment of some verses from the Bible each day.[31] This latter Schempp Decision of 17 June 1963, in which the Supreme Court ruled that Pennsylvania law may not require the reading of at least ten verses from the Holy Bible without comment at the opening of each public school on each school day, has had a somewhat unexpected consequence. Mr. Justice Tom Clark in stating the decision observed that education is not complete without a knowledge of the history of religion, comparative religion, and the Bible. He added: "Nothing that we have said here indicates that such study of the Bible or of religion, when presented objectively as part of a secular program of education, may not be effected consistent with the First Amendment."[32]

A decade earlier a report issued in 1951 by the Educational Policies Commission of the National Educational Association of the US and the American Association of School Administrators stated that there should be teaching about moral and spiritual values in the public schools:

> The American people have rightly expected the schools of this country to teach moral and spiritual values. The schools have accepted this responsibility. . . . No society can survive without a moral order. A system of moral and spiritual values is indispensable to group living.[33]

Ten values were listed: 1) The supreme importance of individual personality. 2) Each person should accept moral responsibility. 3) Institutions are the servants of mankind. 4) Mutual consent is better than violence. 5) The human mind should be liberated by access to information and opinion. 6) Excellence in mind, character, and creative ability should be fostered. 7) All persons should be judged by the same moral standards. 8) Brotherhood should take precedence over selfish interest. 9) Each person should have the greatest possible opportunity for the pursuit of happiness, provided only that such activities do not substantially interfere with the similar opportunities of others. 10) Each person should be offered the emotional and spiritual experiences which transcend the materialistic aspects of life.[34] The Report went on to state:

> American democracy cannot select any system of religious faith as the sole basis for the values to which all Americans subscribe. Nevertheless these moral and spiritual values themselves command, with minor exceptions, the allegiance of all thoughtful Americans. . . . However we may disagree on religious creeds, we can agree on moral and spiritual values. . . . The public schools should teach all children a decent respect for the religious opinions of mankind and the basic facts concerning the role of religion in the history and culture of mankind. . . . There can be no doubt that the American democracy is grounded in a religious tradition. While religion may not be the only source for democratic moral and religious values, it is surely one of the important sources.[35]

III

Given the statements in the Report of the Educational Policies Commission, which are similar to what one finds in Swedish curricular plans, and the opinion of Mr. Justice Clark in the Schempp Decision, that objective study of the Bible or of religion in the public schools can be consistent with the First Amendment, why is there nonetheless such a difference between Swedish and American public education with respect to teaching in this area?[36] The major reason for the difference is that such teaching can be controversial and those who make decisions about curricular matters in American public schools want as much as possible to avoid controversy. A contributing factor is that American public education is extremely decentralized. Each state has its own department of education that sets general standards and administers state aid to local school districts, while more specific decisions about the curriculum are made in the local school district. Local school boards are very responsive to parental pressure, fearful of becoming vulnerable to lawsuits, and worried lest negative community attitudes could result in defeat of referendums to authorize needed additional funding. There are strong reasons, therefore, to avoid any teaching with which parents in the district might not agree.

The situation is quite different, however, in Sweden. There decisions about the curriculum are made and enforced nationally. Recently Sweden's Supreme Administrative Court required the Östergötland County Council to remove wording about Christian ethics it had introduced into the curricular plan for the schools of that county. The County Council was told that in revising the language of the national curricular plan it had exceeded its authority.[37] The court decision did not mean that there was not to be teaching about Christian ethics but that the description of such teaching for the schools of Östergötland County had to correspond to the description in the national curricular plan.

On the American scene how controversial moral education can be, is clearly seen when sex education is considered. Despite the need for such education, given the rise of teen-age pregnancy and the spread of AIDS,[38] it is extremely difficult to introduce this subject into the public school curriculum. Even with sex education being excluded, proponents of a legislative program called "Contract with America," presently being advanced by Republicans in the US House of Representatives, are in effect saying that there is now too much controversial moral education in the public schools. The Contract states that it is through the family that values such as responsibility, morality, commitment, and faith are learned, and that values of the family are under attack from the education establishment. The Contract therefore proposes legislation to "strengthen the rights of parents to protect their children against education programs that undermine the values taught in the home."[39] Pitting families and schools against each other on the issue of moral education is extremely unfortunate, for moral education, whether it is so called or not, cannot successfully be excluded from public education. In Shakespeare's play *The Merchant of Venice*, Shylock has to realize that he cannot cut from Antonio a pound of flesh without also shedding blood. So also religious and ethical questions are implicit throughout all the areas of general education. Moral education should be a cooperative enterprise in which parents, churches and their functional equivalents, and schools all participate. Ways must be found to develop meaningful dialogue on the issues involved so that "culture war" can be avoided.[40]

An important question in this connection is whether all moral education need be prescriptive. In the case of moral norms, such as honesty, respect for human dignity, acceptance of individual responsibility, the school can be prescriptive in its teaching. Norms of this kind are noncontroversial and without there being explicit reference to moral education, there is teaching about them throughout the curriculum. With respect to some other moral issues, differing possible options must be considered. Examples of such issues are: Asking whether national self-interest should be the primary consideration in US relations with Third World nations. Does justice have the same meaning for all US citizens? How can the often claimed right of the individual to bear arms be related to the inviolability of human life? What is meant by human life; when does human life that should be held inviolable begin and when does it end? Is equality between women and men a goal toward which any society should strive? What should be done to remove what remains of discriminatory practices against racial and other minorities? To examine questions of this kind can be controversial. Objectivity here requires that the teaching be factual and as comprehensive as possible.

One way to deal with controversial moral differences is to recognize the extent to which they are rooted in differences in religious faith. If this is to be done, moral education must also include teaching about religion. A helpful way to understand the importance of religion for the common life of a community is to compare the community to a tree. The roots that support the more visible trunk and leafy branches are the differing faiths to be found in the community. That there are several such roots can be a source of strength rather than weakness. The trunk is the de facto moral consensus that enables the citizens to live and work together. This consensus must again and again be renegotiated. The leafy branches are the differences in both religious practice and moral behavior that in a pluralistic society are permitted to flourish. Religious faith that is foundational in any society has a dual relationship with moral behavior. On the one hand, some moral imperatives derive directly from religious faith. It can be helpful in deliberations about moral issues to know how this derivation occurs, why one faith calls for one kind of moral behavior and why another prompts different moral judgments. Another relationship between religious faith and moral behavior, is that faith provides the individual with the motive to do what she/he is persuaded is good or right.

Three distinctively different kinds of motivation for moral behavior are: 1) One is motivated by sanctions, the threat of punishment if one does what is wrong, the hope for reward if one does what is right. While these sanctions here and now are administered

142

by the society in which one lives, one believes that behind them is a transcendent lawgiver, who will ultimately correct earthly sanctions insofar as they are in error and reward or punish either in this life or in a life to come. 2) One is motivated by self-interest and believes the world is so ordered that through diligent effort one's desires for various goods can be satisfied. One conforms to the ethical norms of the community in which one lives in order to be successful in one's striving. With respect to the similar striving of others one may believe that there is an invisible hand that brings forth from the self-interested striving of the many the greatest good of all. There can also be a negative form of this faith. If one is convinced human desire for the most part cannot be satisfied, the appropriate behavior is to curb it and even seek to root it out. 3) One is motivated by gratitude. One believes that one has been loved, by parents and many others, ultimately by the presence in history of a transcendent, redemptive and creative community-forming love. This love defines one's obligations and provides guidance as to how one satisfies one's own desires and responds to the desires of others.[41] These different kinds of motivation represent different ways of answering the fundamental religious question, What do/may I/we believe and hope? The question as formulated implies that one already does believe and hope in some way, but it is also possible that this convictional orientation could change, for there are several viable religious options. The two verbs "believe" and "hope" are needed because we believe in the present (which belief may also involve an interpretation of the past), but we also anticipate with more or less hope the future, no matter how distantly that future may be projected. Many people are not fully conscious of how they are actually answering this fundamental religious question. A part of the educational task is to help them gain self-knowledge at this point. As this is done it is essential to recognize that the religious question can be answered in a number of fundamentally different ways.

It should be possible in public education to examine the possible answers to the religious question, especially as they relate to the possible answers to the ethical question (What should/ought I/we do?). It will be helpful if there is general agreement by all that these questions must in fact be answered by everyone. Just as it is impossible to be amoral, in the sense that one simply ignores the moral question, so, if the religious question is as broadly defined as proposed above, everyone believes and hopes in some way. Since the options suggested above are faith options, no one of them is "true" to

143

the exclusion of the others. They are also rationally incommensurable, there being no common standard in terms of which they can be evaluated. How the options differ can be recognized and each person finds herself/himself believing and hoping in one or another of the ways indicated. At the same time, despite the significant differences between the faith and hope options, and the moral implications derived from them, a de facto moral consensus can be defined so as to make possible communal life. Education in the public sector about religion and ethics can help to define this consensus, thus contributing to the necessary unity communal life requires. It can also have the effect of strengthening particular faith communities. In a religiously pluralistic society there is much to gain if there is objective teaching about religion and ethics both in the public schools and in its various religious communities.

NOTES

[1] G. Everett Arden, *Augustana Heritage: A History of the Augustana Lutheran Church* (Rock Island, Ill.: Augustana Press, 1963), 106.

[2] Knut B. Westman, *Uppsala möte och dess betydelse* (Stockholm: Svenska kyrkans diakonistyrelses bokförlag, 1943), 22.

[3] Much of what follows on the effort to maintain religious unity in Sweden, as well as the subsequent progress toward religious freedom is derived from Åke Andrén, "Religionsfrihet," *Nordisk teologisk uppslagsbok* (hereafter abbreviated as *NTU*), III, 290-293.

[4] Ejje Berling, "Skolväsen," *Svensk uppslagsbok*, vol. 26, 346-348.

[5] Hilding Pleijel, "Pietism," *NTU*, III, 57-63.

[6] William Bredberg, "Svenska Missionsförbundet" and "Paul Peter Waldenström," *NTU*, III, 731-735, 1099-1103.

[7] Birgit Lehndahls, *Religion i skolan - men hur?* (Uppsala: EFS förlaget, 1986), 65-66; Ejje Berling, *op cit.*, 350.

[8] For a summary account of the development in Swedish religious education from 1919-1980, see Birgit Lehndahls, *op. cit.*, 66-67. For a more detailed discussion, see Karl-Göran Algotsson, *Från katekestvång till religionsfrihet. Debatten om religionsundervisningen i skolan under 1900-talet*, Skrifter utgivna av Statsvetenskapliga Föreningen i Uppsala, nr. 70, 1975.

[9] Sven-Åke Selander, *Religionsundervisning för hela människan. Analys av samspelet samhälle, människosyn, innehåll och metoder i religionsundervisningen i Sverige* (Lund: Lunds Universitet, Lärarhögskolan i Malmö, utvecklingsarbete och fältförsök, 22, 1982), 67-68. I wish to express my deep appreciation to Sven-Åke Selander, who has been of great assistance to me in preparing this article, through correspondence and the literature he has sent me. Professor Selander formerly taught at Lund University's Teachers College and now teaches in its Theological Faculty.

[10] Selander, 1982, 99-100. Selander cites the 1962 *läroplan för grundskolan*, 16, 18.

[11] *Läroplan för grundskolan 1980* (Stockholm: Liber UtbildningsFörlaget, 1980), 121.

[12] Arne Lindquist & Jan Wester, *SAMS* (Örebro: Esselte studium, 1987-88), vol. 1-2.

[13] Selander, 1982, 134.

[14] *Läroplan för det obligatoriska skolväsendet och de frivilliga skolformerna*, Lpo-Lpf 94, *Statens skolverks författningssamling* (SKOLFS) 1994.

[15] *Ibid.*, 5.

[16] *Ibid.*, 38-39.

[17] From personal correspondence with Professor Selander, 31 December 1994, and 12 February 1995.

[18] "Harvard University," *Encyclopaedia Britannica*, 1964, vol. 11, 137.

[19] The description is taken from a brief review of *Jamestown: 1544-1699* by Carl Bridenbaugh (Oxford), in *The New Yorker*, vol. 56 (14 April 1980), 175.

[20] Ellwood P. Cubberley, "Education: United States," *Encyclopaedia Britannica*, 1941, vol. 7, 991.

[21] The Constitution of the United States, Amendment 1.

[22] David B. Tyack, "Church-State Relations in Education, History," *The Encyclopedia of Education* (Macmillan and Free Press, 1971), vol. 2, 114.

[23] It can be noted that Massachusetts and Connecticut were two of the three states that failed to ratify the ten amendments that form the Bill of Rights, Massachusetts not doing so until 1941, the 150th anniversary of the Bill of Rights' ratification. Alfred H. Kelley and Winfrid A. Harbison, *The American Constitution, Its Origin and Development*, 4th ed. (New York: W. W. Norton & Co., 1970), 176; Broadus Mitchell and Louise Pearson Mitchell, *A Biography of the Constitution of the United States* (New York: Oxford U. Press, 1964), p. 204.

[24] For a more detailed account of this development, see Sydney E. Ahlstrom, *A Religious History of the American People* (New Haven: Yale U. Press, 1972), 387-403.

[25] William Kailer Dunn, *What Happened to Religious Education?* (Baltimore: Johns Hopkins Press, 1958), 122-126. Raymond B. Culver, *Horace Mann and Religion in the Massachusetts Public Schools* (New Haven: Yale U. Press, 1929), 226-227, states that Dr. Emmons addressed in his funeral sermon the subject of "dying unconverted," implying that this had happened in Stephen's case.

[26] Dunn, *op. cit.*, 104.

[27] *Ibid.*, 141, 149

[28] *Ibid.*, 267-270.

[29] 1948 *Illinois ex rel. McCullum v. Board of Education* (333 U.S. 203).

[30] 1962 *Engel v. Vitale* (370 U.S. 421).

[31] 1963 *School District Abington Township v. Schempp* (374 U.S. 203) and *Murray v. Curlett* (374 U.S. 203).

[32] (374 U.S. 225), 83A, S. Ct. 1573. See Nicholas Woltersdorff, "Religion in the Public Schools," *The Encyclopedia of Education*, vol. 7, 469, and Clark Spurlock, "Supreme Court of the United States and Education," *Ibid.*, vol. 8, 568.

[33] *Moral and Spiritual Values in the Public Schools*, Educational Policies Commission, National Education Association of the US, and the American Association of School Administrators, Washington, DC, 1951, 3. Among the twenty members of the Educational Policies Commission was Dwight D. Eisenhower, then president of Columbia University.

[34] *Ibid.*, 18-29. The elaboration of the eighth value of brotherhood included this statement: "Our ideal is the good Samaritan, rather than the man who asked whether he must be his brother's keeper." 27.

[35] *Ibid.*, 33, 73.

[36] After the Schempp Decision, some efforts were made to introduce objective teaching about religion in some secondary schools. Budgetary restrictions have, however, curtailed these programs in recent years. There has been a greater expansion of religious studies in public universities.

[37] *Sydsvenska dagbladet snällposten*, Malmö, 15 February 1995, A6. This newspaper item was called to my attention by Professor Bo Johnson of the University of Lund.

[38] See "Remarks by Rep. Newt Gingrich," 11 November 1994. *Contract with America*, Ed Gillespie & Bob Schellhas, eds. (New York: Time Books, 1994), 182.

[39] *Ibid.*, 79.

[40] A recent news item stated: "Educators and religious parents fighting a bitter 'culture war' over the future of U.S. public schools signed a pledge in Arlington, Va., to tone down their rhetoric and cooperate for children's good. The agreement won't resolve such issues as prayer in school, teaching creationism and sex education. But the 17 groups—from the Christian Coalition to the People for the American Way—pledged to work to solve disputes before they become lawsuits, improve communication and respect each other's positions." *Star Tribune*, Minneapolis, Minn., 22 March 1995, A7. For a discussion of the phenomenon known as "culture war," see James Davison Hunter, *Culture Wars: The Struggle to Define America* (New York: Basic Books, 1991).

[41] These three patterns of motivation are my interpretation of what Anders Nygren called the nomos, eros, and agape motifs. See Anders Nygren, *Agape and Eros*, rev. trans. Philip S. Watson (Philadelphia: Westminster Press, 1953); Bernhard Erling, *Nature and History: A Study in Theological Methodology with Special Attention to the Method of Motif Research* (Lund: C.W.K. Gleerup, 1960); "Motif Research Analysis and the Existence and Nature of God," *Perspective*, 10 (1969), 155-67.

BIBLIOGRAPHY OF THE PUBLISHED WRITINGS OF DR. CONRAD BERGENDOFF 1963-1995

Compiled by JUDITH BELAN

This bibliography supplements the one compiled by Ernest M. Espelie in *The Swedish Immigrant Community in Transition: Essays in Honor of Dr. Conrad Bergendoff*, published by the Augustana Historical Society, Rock Island, in 1963. The materials cited have been arranged alphabetically in the following categories: I and II, Addenda to the earlier bibliography, including books, articles, translations, and book reviews; III. Books and pamphlets, written or edited; IV. Articles appearing in journals and periodicals; V. Articles and essays in books and yearbooks; VI. Books and articles translated; VII. Books reviewed; and VIII. Selected biographical sketches and works about Conrad Bergendoff.

An extensive bibliography of published and unpublished works is included in the dissertation, "Conrad Bergendoff: the Making of an Ecumenist—a Study in Confessionalism and Ecumenism in Early Twentieth Century American Lutheranism," by Byron Ralph Swanson (Princeton Theological Seminary, 1970). The papers of Conrad Bergendoff, and many of his published works, are available at the Augustana College Library, Special Collections.

I. ADDENDA: BOOKS, ARTICLES, TRANSLATIONS, 1912-1962

"The American Student of 1920," *Augustana Observer*, 18:5-8, Jan. 1920.

"Annual Meeting of the Augustana Foreign Mission Society," *Lutheran Companion*, 28:99, 14 Feb. 1920.

"The Augustana Foreign Mission Society," in *The Missionary Calendar of the Augustana Foreign Mission Society*, v. 1. Rock Island: Augustana Foreign Mission Society, 1921. pp. 85-89.

"Augustana—Synoden och svenskhetens bevarande," *Allsvensk samling*, 11, 15 April 1924.

"Aulén, Gustav Emmanuel Hildebrand," in *An Encyclopedia of Religion*, edited by Vergilius Ferm. New York: The Philosophical Library, 1945, pp. 47-48. Numerous other brief entries throughout. See, e. g. 78-79, 316, 317, 326, 455, 725, 752, 753.

"Bread for the Hungry," *Augustana Observer*, 13:7-10, Jan. 1915.

"C. L. E. Esbjörn—An Appreciation," in *My Church*, v. 25, edited by Carl H. Sandgren. Rock Island: Augustana Book Concern, 1939. pp. 63-66.

"Charles Michael Jacobs," in *My Church*, v. 24, edited by Carl H. Sandgren. Rock Island: Augustana Book Concern, 1938. pp. 77-80.

"Christian Baptism," *The Salem Messenger*, 38:2-3, April 1925.

"The Christian Conscience and Nuclear Warfare," *The National Lutheran*, 30:8,10, Oct. 1962.

"Christian Convention of Augustana Young People," *Lutheran Companion*, 28:733, 13 Nov. 1920.

"Christianity and Christian Science," *The Lutheran Church Review*, 41:59-79, Jan. 1922.

"Comments on Brunner's Essay," *Lutheran World*, 7:271-272, Dec. 1960.

"Educational Relations," in *Preliminary Papers of Commission III, Lutheran World Convention*, Oct. 1939, pp. 26-28.

The Expanding Horizons of the Church. The Christian Growth Series of Sunday School Lessons. Edited by Theodore K. Finck, C. E. Linder, and J. Vincent Nordgren. Teacher's Guide and Study Book, Senior II, Fourth Quarter. Philadelphia: Christian Growth Series, 1949.

"A Faith for These Times," in *A Faith for These Times: Lutheran Sermons for Our Day*, edited by S. J. Sebelius. Rock Island: Augustana Book Concern, 1942. pp. 47-63.

"A Faith that Understands." Inaugural address, Carthage College, Carthage, Illinois, 15 Oct. 1950.

"The Foremost Freedom." Baccalaureate address, Augustana College, Rock Island, 28 May 1944.

"From Generation to Generation." Address to 110th Annual Convention of Central Conference, Rock Island, 26 April 1962.

"From the Connecticut to the Mississippi," *Augustana Observer*, 10:289-291, Dec. 1912.

"The Frontispiece in Our Catechism," *The Church School Teacher*, 2:1, 7-8, 19 Nov. 1933.

"Funeral Address," in *John H. Hauberg, 1869-1955; A Memorial*. 1955. 6 pp. Delivered on 16 Sept. 1955, Rock Island, Illinois.

"The Gospel of Life," in *Preaching the Resurrection*, edited by Alton M. Motter. Philadelphia: Fortress Press, 1959. pp. 1-9.

"The Hope of Missions," *Missions-Tidning*, 15:3-5, April 1921.

"Illinois Conference Luther League," *Lutheran Companion*, 30:119, 25 Feb. 1922.

"In Defense of What?" Guest editorial, *Times-Democrat* (Davenport, Iowa), 27 Sept. 1958, p. 8.

"Lent," *Budbäraren*, 35:1, March 1922.

"The Lutheran Church and Her Sunday School," *Lutheran Companion*, 28:758-759, 775, 790-791, 806-807, 27 Nov., 4, 11 and 18 Dec. 1920.

149

"The Lutheran College and Culture," *Journal of the Association of Lutheran College Faculties*, 2:7-16, Dec. 1949.

"Lutheran Worship," *Budbäraren*, 35:2-4, July 1922.

"Lutheranism," in *A Handbook of Christian Theology*, edited by Marvin Halverson and Arthur Cohen. Cleveland: World Pub. Co., 1958. pp. 220-223.

"Memories and Vision," *Augustana Observer*, 18:135-139, April 1920.

"The Nature and Purpose of the Religious Conference of Young People at Augustana," *Lutheran Companion*, 29:23, 8 Jan. 1921.

"Old Main," *Augustana Bulletin*, ser. 45, no. 12, Dec. 1950, pp. 1-3. Founders' Day address, 27 April 1950.

"On the Thirty-Fourth Anniversary of the Augustana Foreign Mission Society," *Lutheran Companion*, 28:275, 1 May 1920.

"Our Attitude Toward Liturgical Innovations." Pamphlet distributed by Augustana Liturgy Commission, 1946.

"Our Literary Societies," *Augustana Observer*, 12:33-35, May 1914.

"Our Teachers," *Rockety-I*, Rock Island, 1915, p. 22.

"Our Youth for Christ," in *The Master and Augustana Youth*, edited by Evald Lawson. Rock Island: Augustana Book Concern, 1926. pp. 147-153.

"Past and Present," *Augustana Observer*, 18:226-227, Sept. 1920.

"Pastor's Reports," *Budbäraren*, vols. 36-37 (for the years 1922-1923), and *The Salem Messenger*, vols. 38-44 (for the years 1924-1929).

"Public Sentiment," *Augustana Observer*, 12:4-5, March 1914. Delivered in an oratorical contest under the auspices of The Prohibition League.

"The Radiant Life," in *Conference Echo: The "Radiant Life" Conference*, edited by Carl Segerhammar. Rock Island: Augustana Book Concern, 1929.

"The Removal and Reconstruction of Salem," in *A Historical Record of Salem Lutheran Church*, edited by H. C. Nelson. Chicago, 1943, pp. 28-37.

"The Role of the University," *Campus Lutheran*, 5:2-4, 6, 22-23, Jan. 1954.

"Salutatory," *Augustana Observer*, 13:3-4, May 1915.

"The Secular Idea of Progress and the Christian Doctrine of Sanctification," *The Augustana Quarterly*, 12:53-70, Jan. 1933.

"Söderblom, Lars Olaf Jonathan (Nathan)," in *Encyclopedia of Religion*, edited by Vergilius Ferm. New York: Philosophical Library, 1945. p. 725.

"Some Values of Athletics," *Augustana Observer*, 18:45-46, Feb. 1920.

"The Soul of a Church School," *Augustana Bulletin*, alumni issue, ser. 27, no. 1, Jan. 1932, p. 3.

"The Source of Authority," *Lutheran Companion*, 108:16, 15 Aug. 1962.

"The Sphere of Revelation," *The Harvard Divinity School Bulletin*, no. 14, 25 April 1949, pp. 21-34. Delivered as Dudleian Lecture at Harvard, 6 April 1948. Also published in *The Lutheran World Review*, 1:38-53, Oct. 1948.

"Spiritual Growth," *Lutheran Companion*, 30:169-170, 18 March 1922.

"$10,000 for Salem," *Budbäraren*, 35:3, Feb. 1922.

"Their Faith They Brought with Them from the Old World to the New," in *This Is My Church*, edited by John R. Nyberg. Rock Island:

Augustana Book Concern, 1960. pp. 8-9.

"Theological Education," [Part 6, "Religious Resources and Obligations of the Church-Related College: A Symposium"], *Christian Education*, 22:188-190, Feb. 1939.

"To the Members of Salem, October 22, 1922," *Budbäraren* 35:2, Nov. 1922.

"Tree Planting," *Budbäraren* 36:2, Nov. 1923.

"The Under-Developed Areas of the Human Mind," in *The Small College Annual*, 1955, pp. 6-7.

"The Unique Character of the Reformation in Sweden," in *The Symposium on Seventeenth-Century Lutheranism*, edited by A. C. Piepkorn, R. D. Preus, and E. L. Leuker, v. 1. St. Louis: The Symposium on Seventeenth-Century Lutheranism, 1962, pp. 91-105.

"Vid L. P. Esbjörns grav," *Augustana*, 71:726, 18 Nov. 1926.

"Westphalia, Amsterdam and America," *American Association of Theological Schools Bulletin*, 18:67-74, June 1948.

"What About Lutheran Unity in America?" *Frontiers*, 8:6-9, May 1957.

"What Is True Faith?" *Budbäraren*, 35:1-3, Feb. 1922.

"What Think the Alumni of Augustana?" *Augustana Observer*, 18:26, Jan. 1920.

"Who's Who—And a New Science Building," *Augustana Observer*, 18:114, March 1920.

Wingren, Gustav. "The Christian's Calling According to Luther," translated by Conrad Bergendoff. *Augustana Quarterly*, 21:3-16, Jan. 1942.

"Within the Church," *Budbäraren*, 34:2, Aug. 1921.

II. ADDENDA: BOOK REVIEWS, 1930-1960

Acton, Lord. *Essays on Freedom and Power*. The Lutheran Quarterly, 1:106-107, Feb. 1949.

Allard, F. M. *Från Luther till Bach*. Augustana Quarterly, 13:285-286, July 1934.

Ander, O. F. T. N. *Hasselquist: The Career and Influence of a Swedish-American Clergyman, Journalist, and Educator*. Augustana Quarterly, 11:259-266, July 1932.

Andrén, Åke. *Introductorium Theologicum*. The Lutheran Quarterly, 4:103-104, Feb. 1952.

Aulén, Gustaf. *The Faith of the Christian Church*. Theology Today, 6:116-118, April 1949.

Bainton, Roland. *The Reformation of the Sixteenth Century*. The Lutheran Quarterly, 5:97, Feb. 1953.

Borgenstierna, Gert. *Arbetarteologi och altarteologi*. Lutheran Quarterly, 5:225, May 1953.

Brilioth, Yngve. *Nattvarden i evangeliskt gudstjänstliv*. The Lutheran Quarterly, 3:412, Nov. 1951.

Clark, E. T., editor, with W. G. Cram. *The Book of Daily Devotions*. Augustana Quarterly, 12:87-89, Jan. 1933.

Dillenberger, John. *God Hidden and Revealed*. Theology Today, 10:556-558, Jan. 1954.

Estborn, Sigfrid. *Under Guds grepp. En studie i Nathan Söderbloms förkunnelse*. Augustana Quarterly, 24:274-275, July 1945.

Ferm, Vergilius, editor. *Contemporary American Theology*, v. 1-2. *Augustana Quarterly*, 12:371-372, Oct. 1933.

Flew, Newton. *The Idea of Perfection in Christian Theology*. *Augustana Quarterly*, 14:180-182, April 1935.

Helander, Dick, editor. *Bönbok*. *Augustana Quarterly*, 12:87-89, Jan. 1933.

Hofrenning, B. M. *Captain Jens Munk's Septentrionalis*. *Augustana Quarterly*, 24:268, July 1945.

Hök, Gösta. *Herrnhutisk teologi i svensk gestalt*. *The Lutheran Quarterly*, 3:231-232, May 1951.

Holmquist, Hjalmar. *Handbok i svensk kyrkohistoria*, II, III. *The Lutheran Quarterly*, 8:86, Feb. 1956.

Holmquist, Hjalmar. *Svenska kyrkans historia*. *Augustana Quarterly*, 13:284-285, July 1934.

Holmström, Folke. *Det eskatologiska motivet. Nutida teologi*. *Augustana Quarterly*, 14:355-356, Oct. 1935.

Horton, Walter M. *Toward a Reborn Church*. *The Lutheran Quarterly*, 2:102, Feb. 1950.

Institute of Social and Religious Research. *The Education of American Ministers*, 4 v. *Augustana Quarterly*, 13:173-175, Apr. 1934.

Joyce, G. H. *Christian Marriage—An Historical and Doctrinal Study*. *Augustana Quarterly*, 13:374-377, Oct. 1934.

Karlström, Nils. *Ekumeniska preludier*. *The Lutheran Quarterly*, 3:326, Aug. 1951.

Kerr, Hugh Thompson. *A Compend of Luther's Theology*. *Christendom*, 9:109-110, Winter 1944.

King, W. P., editor. *Behaviorism, a Battle Line. Augustana Quarterly,* 10:77-78, Jan. 1931.

Krumbine, M. H., editor. *The Process of Religion. Augustana Quarterly,* 13:87-91, Jan. 1934.

Kyrka och folkbildning. The Lutheran Quarterly, 2:221-222, May 1950.

Lindroth, Hjalmar. *Recent Theological Research in Sweden: A Luther Renaissance. The Lutheran Quarterly,* 3:106-107, Feb. 1951.

Liturgical Society of St. James. *Pro Ecclesia Lutherana,* v. 1. *Augustana Quarterly,* 13:165-167, April 1934.

Liturgical Society of St. James. *Pro Ecclesia Lutherana,* v. 2. *Augustana Quarterly,* 14:281-282, July 1935.

Löwith, Karl. *Meaning in History. The Lutheran Quarterly,* 1:472-473, Nov. 1949.

Luther Academy in Sonderhausen. *Nachrichten den Luther—Akademie in Sonderhausen. Augustana Quarterly,* 14:187-188, April 1935.

McConnell, J. C. *Christianity and Coercion. Augustana Quarterly,* 13:87-91, Jan. 1934.

McNeill, J. T. *Unitive Protestantism. Augustana Quarterly,* 18:166-167, Apr. 1939.

Malmeström, Elis. *J. A. Eklund. En biografi. The Lutheran Quarterly,* 3:112, Feb. 1951.

Melanchthon, Phillip. *The Loci Communes of Phillip Melanchthon.* Translation by Charles L. Hill. *The Journal of Religion,* 26:141-142, April 1946.

Moffatt, James. *The Days Before Yesterday. Augustana Quarterly,* 10:86-87, Jan. 1931.

Moffatt, James. *Grace in the New Testament.* Augustana Quarterly, 11:170-174, April 1932.

Moffatt, James. *Love in the New Testament.* Augustana Quarterly, 9:357-362, Oct. 1930.

Morrison, C. C. *The Social Gospel and the Christian Cultus.* Augustana Quarterly, 13:87-91, Jan. 1934.

Morrison, Charles Clayton. *The Unfinished Reformation.* The Lutheran Quarterly, 5:319-320, Aug. 1953.

Mott, John R. *The Present-Day Summons to the World Mission of Christianity.* Augustana Quarterly, 11:85-86, Jan. 1932.

Murray, Robert. *Olavus Petri.* The Lutheran Quarterly, 5:97-98, Feb. 1953.

Newman, Ernst. *Den waldenströmska försoningsläran i historisk belysning.* Augustana Quarterly, 11:259-266, July 1932.

Norberg, Arvid. *Frikyrklighetens uppkomst.* The Lutheran Quarterly, 5:411-412, Nov. 1953.

Nygren, Anders. *Kristus och hans kyrka.* The Lutheran Quarterly, 8:370-371, Nov. 1956.

Odell, Arthur. *Nya Testament på svenska 1526.* Augustana Quarterly, 16:180-181, Apr. 1937.

Opperman, C. J. A. *The English Missionaries in Sweden and Finland.* Church History, 7:196-197, June 1938.

Ottersberg, Gerhard. *Wartburg College, 1852-1952, a Centennial History.* The Lutheran Quarterly, 5:101-102, Feb. 1953.

Pauck, W. *Karl Barth.* Augustana Quarterly, 11:84-85, Jan. 1932.

Pleijel, Hilding. *Från hustavlans tid. Kyrkohistoriska folklivsstudier.* *The Lutheran Quarterly*, 4:237-238, May 1952.

Pleijel, Hilding. *Der Schwedische Pietismus in Seinen Beziehungen zu Deutschland.* *Augustana Quarterlty*, 16:186-187, Apr. 1937.

Pleijel, Hilding. *Svenska kyrkans historia.* *Augustana Quarterly*, 14:275-276, July 1935.

Roos, M. Fr. *Kristlig husandaktsbok.* *Augustana Quarterly*, 12:87-89, Jan. 1933.

Roth, Erick. *Sakrament nach Luther.* *The Lutheran Quarterly*, 5:100-101, Feb. 1953.

Rutenber, Culbert G. *The Dagger and the Cross: An Examination of Christian Pacifism.* *Lutheran Quarterly*, 3:116, Feb. 1951.

Schweitzer, Albert. *The Philosophy of Civilization.* *The Lutheran Quarterly*, 2:230-231, May 1950.

Smith, A. F., editor. *Talking with God.* *Augustana Quarterly*, 12:87-89, Jan. 1933.

Society of St. Ambrose. *The Use of the Common Service.* *Augustana Quarterly*, 14:282-283, July 1935.

Söderblom, Nathan. *Ett år. Ord för varje dag.* *Augustana Quarterly*, 12:87-89, Jan. 1933.

Stephenson, George M. *The Religious Aspects of Swedish Immigration.* *Augustana Quarterly*. 11:259-266, July 1932.

Tappert, Theodore G. and John W. Doberstein. *Notebook of a Colonial Clergyman.* *The Lutheran Quarterly*, 12:354-355, Nov. 1960.

Tidskrift for kyrkomusik och svenskt gudstjänstliv. *Augustana Quarterly*, 14:282-283, July 1935.

Tomkins, Oliver S. *The Church in the Purpose of God*. *Lutheran Quarterly*, 4:220, May 1952.

Van Dusen, Henry P. *God in These Times*. *Augustana Quarterly*, 14:353-355, Oct. 1935.

Westin, G. *Svenska kyrkan och de protestantiska enhetssträvandena under 1630-talet*. *Augustana Quarterly*, 18:166-167, Apr. 1939.

III. BOOKS AND PAMPHLETS WRITTEN OR EDITED, 1963-1990

Augustana . . . a Profession of Faith: A History of Augustana College, 1860-1935. Rock Island: Augustana College Library, 1969. xi, 220 pp. (Publication no. 33).

The Augustana Ministerium: A Study of the Careers of the 2,504 Pastors of the Augustana Evangelical Lutheran Synod/Church, 1860-1962. Rock Island: Augustana Historical Society, 1980. 246 pp. (Publication no. 28).

The Church of Sweden on the Delaware, 1638-1831. Rock Island: Augustana Historical Society, 1988. 38 pp. (Publication no. 37). "A revised and expanded version . . . of an article that originally appeared in *Church History*, Volume 7, September, 1938."

The Church of the Lutheran Reformation: A Historical Survey of Lutheranism. St. Louis: Concordia Publishing House, 1967. xv, 339 pp.

A History of the Augustana Library, 1860-1990: An International Treasure. Rock Island: Augustana Historical Society, 1990. 48 pp. (Publication no. 39).

The Lutheran Church in America and Theological Education: A Report to the Board of Theological Education. New York: Lutheran Church in America, The Board of Theological Education, Nov. 1963. 48 pp. Dr. Bergendoff was the first executive secretary of the Board of

Theological Education of the Lutheran Church in America.

Olavus Petri and the Ecclesiastical Transformation in Sweden, 1521-1552: A Study in the Swedish Reformation. Philadelphia: Fortress Press, 1965. xvi, 267 pp. New introduction by Conrad Bergendoff, xi-xvi. Submitted as Ph.D. thesis at University of Chicago in 1928; published by Macmillan in 1928. Reviewed in Swedish by Sven Ingebrand in *Kyrkohistorisk årsskrift*, Uppsala, 1993.

One Hundred Years of Oratorio at Augustana: A History of the Handel Oratorio Society, 1881-1980. Rock Island: Augustana Historical Society, 1981. 54 pp. (Publication no. 29).

IV. ARTICLES APPEARING IN JOURNALS AND PERIODICALS, 1963-1995

"AHS: To Celebrate the Stories; the Old Main Chapel," *Augustana College Magazine*, Winter 1983, p. 11.

"After Twenty-Five Years," *Lutheran World*, 19:343-354, 1972. On the twenty-fifth anniversary of the Lutheran World Federation.

"An Ancient Culture in a New Land," *Swedish Pioneer Historical Quarterly*, 27:127-134, April 1976.

"The Arts and a College Education," *Augustana Historical Society Newsletter*, 4:13-15, Spring/Summer 1989. Address at the opening of a Carl Milles Exhibit, Centennial Hall Gallery, Augustana College, 5 March 1989.

"Augustana—A People's Aspiration," *The Cresset*, 39:6-10, Feb. 1976.

"Augustana—a Profession of Faith," *Augustana College Alumni Bulletin*, ser. 64, no. 11, Fall 1969, pp. 13-15.

"Augustana and Her Relatives," *Concordia Historical Institute Quarterly*, 57:162-166, Winter 1984.

"Augustana College—A Century-Old Bridge Builder," *The Bridge* (Karlstad, Sweden), 14:40-41, 58-59, 1982.

"Augustana in America and Sweden," *Swedish Pioneer Historical Quarterly*, 24:238-241, Oct. 1973.

"The Augustana Pastor: Saga of a Thousand Immigrants from Sweden," *Swedish Pioneer Historical Quarterly*, 31:34-50, Jan. 1980.

"The Beginnings of the Swedish Pioneer Centennial," *Swedish Pioneer Historical Quarterly*, 20:161-169, Oct. 1969.

"Bergendoffs Visit Broneer in Corinth," *Augustana College Bulletin*, alumni no., ser. 66, no. 10, Fall 1971, p. 7.

"Beyond Skepticism," *Augustana College Magazine*, July 1981, pp. 12-13. Commencement address, Augustana College, 1981, on the pursuit of peace.

"Beyond the Horizon," *Augustana College Bulletin*, alumni no., ser. 58, no. 4, Summer 1963, p. 7. Excerpts from the baccalaureate sermon, Augustana, 2 June 1963.

"A Century of College and Community Cooperation," *Augustana College Bulletin*, ser. 70, no. 1, Jan. 1975, pp. 7-8.

"A Century of Science at Augustana," *Augustana College Bulletin*, April 1979, pp. 3-6.

"A Century-Old Monument: Augustana College's Old Main," *Swedish American Historical Quarterly*, 35:267-281, July 1984.

"The Challenge of Vatican II," *Valparaiso University Bulletin*, 41:55-62, 22 Sept. 1967. Gross Memorial Lecture, delivered at Valparaiso University, 1967.

"Delivered from Sleep and Damnation; a Meditation for Lent," *Lutheran Women*, 6:6-9, March 1968. Condensed from address titled

"The Mission of the Lutheran Church," delivered at the Lutheran Mission Conference, Chicago, 7 Nov. 1967.

"The Founders of Augustana," *Augustana College Alumni Bulletin*, ser. 64, no. 8, Summer 1969, pp. 19-21.

"The Future of Luther in Lutheranism," *Lutheran Forum*, 1:8-11, July 1967.

"A Goodly Heritage," *Lutheran Forum*, 22:6, Pentecost 1988. An essay in honor of Glenn C. Stone.

"Guardians of the Past, or Pioneers of the Future," *National Lutheran Educational Conference News Bulletin*. March-April 1964, pp. 1-3. Delivered at the annual meeting of the National Lutheran Educational Conference. Also published in *Creative Tensions; Papers Presented at the Proceedings of the 50th Annual Meeting of the National Lutheran Educational Conference*. Washington, D. C.: National Lutheran Educational Conference, 1964, 28-30.

"In Search of Self," *Swedish Pioneer Historical Quarterly*, 30:87-93, April 1979.

"Luther and Lutheranism Today," *The Catholic World*, 206:63-67, Nov. 1967.

"The Meandering of an Historian," *Concordia Historical Institute Quarterly*, 55:181-184, Winter 1982.

"Nathan Söderblom, Archbishop and Evangelical Catholic," *Una Sancta*, 22:2-17, Trinity 1965.

"No Royal Road," *Augustana College Alumni Bulletin*, ser. 63, no. 8, Summer 1968, pp. 2-5. A chapel talk on the retirement of three Augustana professors, 17 May 1968.

"On the Fortieth Anniversary of the Augustana Historical Society," *Swedish Pioneer Historical Quarterly*, 22:202-211, Oct. 1971.

"A Productive Half Century," *The Bridge* (Karlstad, Sweden), 13:106-108, 1981.

"Publishing Achievements Mark Society's 50 Years of Service," *Swedish Council News*, 5:16-18, Winter 1979.

"Retrospect and Prospect," *The Lutheran Quarterly*, 26:376-382, Nov. 1974.

"Scripture and Tradition at Montreal," *Ho Ellenos* (Greek title transcribed), Central Lutheran Theological Seminary, Fremont, Nebraska, 1:14-15, 21, Spring-Summer 1964.

"The Sender and the Sent," *World Encounter*, 5:7-9, July 1968.

"Shared Time for Religious Education," *Lutheran Education*, 99:290-298, March 1964. Views of Dr. Bergendoff, William A. Kramer, and Neil G. McCluskey.

"Singing the Lord's Song in a New Land," *Lutheran Forum*, 15:16-18, Reformation 1981.

"Some Observations on the Constitution of the Lutheran World Federation," *Lutheran World*, 11:201-203, April 1964.

"The Swedish Element in America," *Illinois Journal of Education*, 61:68-70, April 1970.

"The Swedish Immigrant and the American Way," *Swedish Pioneer Historical Quarterly*, 19:143-157, July 1968.

"A Swedish University Tradition in America," *Swedish-American Historical Quarterly*, 44:4-20, Jan. 1993. Reprinted by the Augustana Historical Society.

"Things, Tools and Thoughts," *Augustana College Bulletin*, Alumni no., ser. 60, no. 8, July 1965, p. 7. Excerpts from the 1965 commencement address at Augustana College.

"The Throne and the Faculties," *The Seminary Review*, Lutheran School of Theology, Rock Island Campus, 18:1-6, Second Quarter 1966.

"Who Wants to Be a Missionary Now?" *The Lutheran Standard*, 9:13-14, 18 Feb. 1969.

"Why Fear the Future?" *Event*, 11:29-31, Dec. 1971.

V. ARTICLES AND ESSAYS IN BOOKS AND YEARBOOKS, 1963-1991

"Augustana—a People in Transition," in *The Swedish Immigrant Community in Transition: Essays in Honor of Dr. Conrad Bergendoff*, edited by J. Iverne Dowie and Ernest M. Espelie. Rock Island: Augustana Historical Society, 1963. pp. 197-208.

"Augustana College," in *The Encyclopedia of the Lutheran Church*, v. 2, edited by Julius Bodensieck. Minneapolis: Augsburg Pub. Co., 1965. p. 1130.

"The Augustana Vision," in *The Augustana Heritage Endowment*. Chicago: Lutheran School of Theology at Chicago, 1991. pp. 5-13.

"Church," in *The Encyclopedia of the Lutheran Church*, v. 1, edited by Julius Bodensieck. Minneapolis: Augsburg Pub. Co., 1965. pp. 486-492.

"The Consolation of the Humanities," in [Papers read at the Henriette C. K. Naeseth Fellowship Dinners] Rock Island: Augustana College, April 1974. pp. 1-7. Paper delivered in April 1970.

"Daily Devotions: December 25-January 1," in *The Word in Season*. Rock Island: Fortress Press, 1965.

"Daily Devotions: November 23-29," in *The Word in Season*. Philadelphia: Fortress Press, 1969.

"The Ecumenical Movement in the Churches," in *Contemporary Club Papers*. Davenport, Iowa. 68:1-10, 1965. Address delivered 22 March 1965.

"The Educational Implications of Christian Faith," in *Some Perspectives on Christian Higher Education*. Washington, D. C.: National Lutheran Educational Conference, April 1964. pp. 17-22. Also published in *Creative Tensions; Papers Presented at the Proceedings of the 50th Annual Meeting of the National Lutheran Educational Conference*. Washington, D. C.: National Lutheran Educational Conference, 1964. pp. 64-69.

"The Ethical Thought of Einar Billing," in *The Scope of Grace: Essays on Nature and Grace in Honor of Joseph Sittler*, edited by Philip J. Hefner. Philadelphia: Fortress Press, 1964. pp. 279-306.

"Faith and Knowledge," in *The Parkander Papers: A Festschrift Honoring Dr. Dorothy J. Parkander*, edited by Jane Telleen, Ann Boaden, and Roald Tweet. Rock Island: East Hall Press and Augustana College Library, 1988. pp. 83-86.

"From Generation to Generation," in *Century +; Salem Lutheran Church, Chicago, Illinois*, edited by Roger Carlson. Chicago, Salem Lutheran Church, 1968. pp. 12-16. Dr. Bergendoff was pastor of Salem Lutheran Church, 1921-1931.

"The Grace Congregation," in *St. John's Remembered*, edited by Ann Boaden. Rock Island: St. John's Lutheran Church, 1988. pp. 4-7. Dr. Bergendoff has been a member of St. John's continuously since 1931.

"An Invocation for the Opening of the New Library," in *conTEXTS; a Celebration of the Augustana College Library*, edited by Lawrence Falbe and Wendy Anderson. Rock Island: East Hall Press, 1991. p. 1. Also in *Augustana College Magazine*, Winter 1990, p. 37.

"Justification and Sanctification: Liturgy and Ethics," in *Marburg Revisited*, edited by Paul C. Empie and James I. McCord. Minneapolis: Augsburg Pub. House, 1965. pp. 118-127. Also separately published jointly by representatives of the North American Area of the World Alliance of Reformed Churches Holding the Presbyterian Order and the U. S. A. National Committee of the Lutheran World Federation. New York: 1965 (A Reexamination of Lutheran and Reformed Traditions, No. 3).

"Living on an Inheritance," in *Seven Sermons from the 125th Anniversary Year of Augustana College, Rock Island, Ill.*, edited by Phil Schroeder. Rock Island: Augustana Campus Ministry and Augustana Historical Society, 1986. pp. 21-23.

"Lutheran Church in America," in *American-Swedish Handbook*, v. 7. Rock Island: Augustana Swedish Institute, 1965. pp. 80-82.

"Peace and the Christian Citizen," in *Amicus Dei: Essays on Faith and Friendship*, edited by Philip J. Anderson. Chicago: Covenant Publications, 1988. pp. 192-199. Paper presented at a Peace Seminar of the Illinois Synod of the Lutheran Church in America, Moline, Ill., 15 Sept. 1984. Also published in *Covenant Quarterly*, 46:192-199, May-Aug. 1988.

"The Relationship between Evangelism and Education in the Mission of the Church," in *Christianity and African Education: The Papers of a Conference at the University of Chicago*, edited by R. Pierce Beaver. Grand Rapids, Michigan: W. B. Eerdmans Pub. Co., 1966. pp. 15-30.

"The Role of Augustana in the Transplanting of a Culture Across the Atlantic," in *The Immigration of Ideas: Studies in the North Atlantic Community: Essays Presented to O. Fritiof Ander*, edited by J. Iverne Dowie and J. Thomas Tredway. Rock Island: Augustana Historical Society, 1968. pp. 67-83 (Publication no. 21).

"The Uniting Word," in *Preaching on Pentecost and Christian Unity*, edited by Alton M. Motter. Philadelphia: Fortress Press, 1965. pp. 10-17.

"Vision and Mission: Ecumenical Perspectives," in *Council of Churches/Churches United of Scott County, Iowa and Rock Island County, Illinois*. 1982. Address at the 21st anniversary celebration, 21 Jan. 1982.

VI. BOOKS AND ARTICLES TRANSLATED, 1964-1994

Aulén, Gustav, "Nathan Söderblom as Theologian," *Una Sancta,* 24:15-30, March 1967. Translated by Conrad Bergendoff.

Enander, Johan A., "Autobiography," in the article "A Significant Enander Document," *Swedish Pioneer Historical Quarterly,* 21: 7-25, Jan. 1970. Introduction, pp. 5-6.

Letters from Andover to Högarp, Sweden, 1858-1898, edited and translated from Swedish by Conrad Bergendoff. Andover: Jenny Lind Chapel Fund, 1988. (Augustana College Library Occasional Paper, no. 17) 53 pp.

Mauritzson, Jules, "Christmas Customs—Old and New," *Augustana Historical Society Newsletter,* 4:3-14, Fall-Winter, 1988-1989. Translated by Conrad Bergendoff. One of three essays published in *Looking West.*

Mauritzson, Jules. *Looking West: Three Essays on Swedish-American Life.* Translated by Conrad Bergendoff. Edited by Ann Boaden and Dag Blanck. Rock Island: Augustana Historical Society, 1994. (Publication no. 42) xviii, 73 pp.

Rönnegard, Sam. "The Augustana Bell Tower," [poem] Preface and translation by Conrad Bergendoff, in *The Augustana Heritage Endowment.* Chicago: Lutheran School of Theology at Chicago, 1991. p. 35. Originally published as "Klockstapeln vid Augustana" in *Utvandrarnas kyrka.* Stockholm: Diakonistyrelsens Bokförlag, 1961.

VII. BOOKS REVIEWED, 1963-1994

Curtis, Charles J. *Nathan Söderblom: Theologian of Revelation. Swedish Pioneer Historical Quarterly,* 18:50-51, Jan. 1967.

Dahl, K. G. William. *Letters Home from the Prairie Priest,* translated by Earl Helge Byleen. *Augustana Historical Society Newsletter,* 9: 11-15, Spring/Summer 1994.

Ingebrand, Sven. *Olavus Petri's reformatoriska åskådning.* *Lutheran Quarterly,* 16:376, Nov. 1964.

Lindbeck, George A. *Dialogue on the Way. Minister's Information Service* (Lutheran Church in America), Jan. 1966, p. 1.

McSorley, Harry M. *Luther: Right or Wrong? An Ecumenical-Theological Study of Luther's Major Work, The Bondage of the Will. Lutheran Forum,* 3:25-26, June 1969.

Maier, Hans. *Revolution und Kirche: Studien zur Fruhgeschichte der christlichen Demokratie (1789-1901). The Annals of the American Academy of Political and Social Science,* 362:204-205, Nov. 1965.

Söderblom, Nathan. *The Nature of Revelation. The Lutheran Quarterly,* 20:100-101, Feb. 1968.

Till, Barry. *The Churches' Search for Unity. Lutheran Forum,* 7:43-44, Feb. 1973.

Van Dusen, Henry P. *Dag Hammarskjöld: The Statesman and His Faith. Swedish Pioneer Historical Quarterly,* 18:176-178, Jan. 1967.

VIII. BIOGRAPHICAL SKETCHES AND WORKS ABOUT CONRAD BERGENDOFF

Bergendoff, Conrad. Interview with Conrad J. Bergendoff on 22-23 June 1977, by Glenn C. Stone. Archives of Cooperative Lutheranism, Lutheran Council in the USA, pp. 1-107.

Bergendoff, Conrad. Interview with Conrad J. Bergendoff on 4 Oct. 1979, by Glenn C. Stone. Archives of Cooperative Lutheranism, Lutheran Council in the USA, pp. 108-143.

Carlson, Edgar M. "Dr. Bergendoff—Christian Scholar and Educator," in *The Swedish Immigrant Community in Transition: Essays in Honor of Dr. Conrad Bergendoff.* Rock Island: Augustana Historical Society,

1963. pp. 209-217.

"Conrad Bergendoff," in *Great Swedish Heritage Awards Night, October 24, 1980*. Minneapolis. pp. 18-19.

"Conrad John Immanuel Bergendoff," in *Profiles in Leadership*. Rock Island: Quest Publishing, 1981. pp. 20-25.

"'Dr. B' Honored," *Augustana College Alumni Bulletin*, ser. 61, no. 1, Winter 1966, p. 11.

"Olmsted, Bergendoff: 75-year Grads," *Augustana College Magazine*, Summer 1990. p. 20.

"Professors of Faith, 1935-1975," *Augustana College Magazine*, Fall 1985, pp. 18-24. About Conrad Bergendoff and several other Augustana professors.

"Q-C Mayors Note 'Bergendoff Day.'" *Augustana College Magazine*, Spring 1989, pp. 14-15.

Swanson, Byron Ralph. "Conrad Bergendoff: the Making of an Ecumenist—a Study in Confessionalism and Ecumenism in Early Twentieth Century American Lutheranism." 403 pp. Thesis (Th.D.) Princeton Theological Seminary, 1970.